Strar ... Camino

Guy,
Thanks for all your support – & your friendship across the miles.

[signature]
08 MAY 2014

Vijitha Yapa Publications
Unity Plaza, 2 Galle Road, Colombo 4, Sri Lanka
Tel. (94 11) 2596960 Fax (94 11) 2594717
e-mail: vijiyapa@gmail.com
www.srilankanbooks.com
www.vijithayapa.com

ISBN 978-955-665-229-1

First Edition May 2014

Printed by Saveco Printing and Packaging, Boralesgamuwa

Strangers on The Camino

A Father, a Son – and a Holy Trail

Sanjiva Wijesinha

VIJITHA YAPA PUBLICATIONS
www.vijithayapa.com

Praise for *'Strangers on the Camino'*

I enjoyed this account of Sanjiva's long walk with his son Shivantha so much. It was a real pleasure to 'walk' the Camino again with both of them and those they met as company.

This book will be of interest and of use to those who are thinking of setting off on their own Camino. The detailed descriptions of the road itself and of the *refugios* as well as the private accommodation give a real sense of what it is like to walk 800 kms over 6 weeks or so.

'Strangers on the Camino' reminds us all that walking slowly, for a long way, is a very good reason to take time out of our hurried lives. Even better if you can do it in the company of someone you love.

Karen Manwaring
Author of *A Slow Walk Across Spain*

A fascinating, entertaining account of a trek along the 800km Camino that is replete with interesting snippets and anecdotes about the rich ethnic, cultural, military and religious history of Spain - this is no ordinary travelogue.

And *Strangers* is even more. The soul-searching, often-exhausting Camino experience reinforced the strong emotional ties between the father and son who began – and completed – this gruelling trek

As you make your own armchair hike through the book, you will meet the many strangers of myriad nationalities and backgrounds they befriended along the way - and discover the many acts of kindness and generosity they encountered.

You will certainly enjoy walking 'The Walk' with these *Strangers on The Camino.*

Roger Thiedeman
Assistant Editor, *Airways*

Sanjiva Wijesinha has utilized his reputable writing flair to give the reader a meticulous insight and perspective of his challenging journey with his son along the Camino of Santiago. It is no surprise that he sets out to educate the reader.

The book's sub-title *'A father, a son – and a holy trail'* is an interesting and spiritual paraphrasing of the fundamental Christian creed of the Blessed Trinity. He thus heralds the way for a very open unbiased study of a religion relatively unfamiliar to him.

The book's content reflects keen observation typical of a surgeon general practitioner with a perspective of the environment, the indigenous people, fellow travellers, fruits of the land, budgeting - plus the hardships, highlights and human touches. He weaves a touch of philosophical flair with an outline of twelve lessons learned from the experience in sharing the journey with his son.

This is an interesting most readable book that would be a valuable read for the prospective pilgrim curious to know what awaits in Northern Spain

John Murtagh
Emeritus Professor of General Practice, Monash University

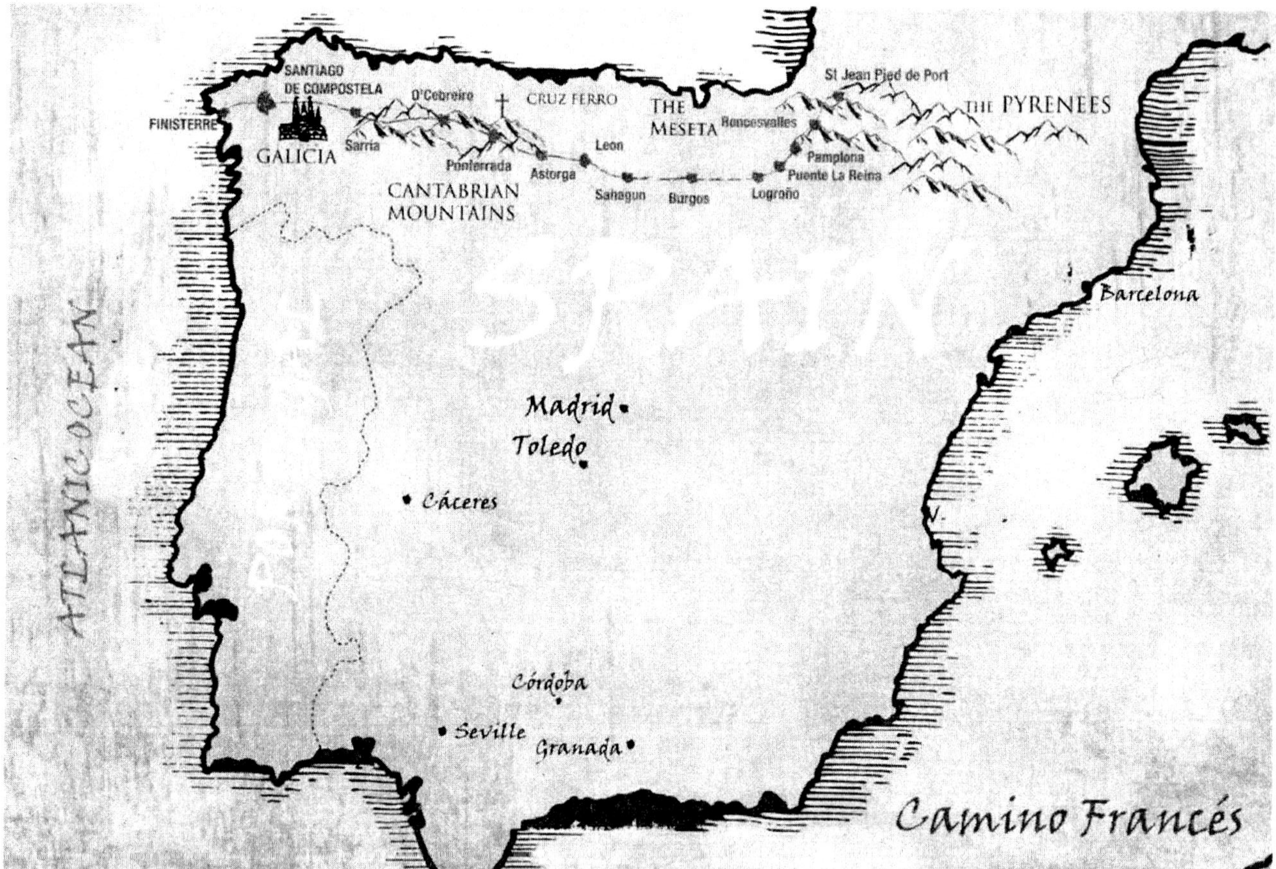

SANTIAGO DE COMPOSTELA
FINISTERRE
GALICIA
Sarria
O'Cebreiro
CRUZ FERRO
Ponferrada
Astorga
Leon
CANTABRIAN MOUNTAINS
THE MESETA
Sahagun
Burgos
Logroño
Roncesvalles
St Jean Pied de Port
Pamplona
Puente La Reina
THE PYRENEES
SPAIN
Barcelona
ATLANTIC OCEAN
Madrid
Toledo
Cáceres
Córdoba
Seville
Granada
Camino Francés

Dedication

To my father - and my son's grandfather -

Sam Wijesinha

Contents

Chronology – where we were each evening

- 14th April 2011: Colombo, Sri Lanka
- 15th April 2011: Paris, France
- 16th April 2011: Bordeaux
- 17th April 2011: St Jean Pied de Port
- 18th April 2011: St Jean Pied de Port
- 19th April 2011: Orisson
- 20th April 2011: Roncesvalles, Spain
- 21st April 2011: Zubiri
- 22nd April 2011: Pamplona
- 23rd April 2011: Pamplona
- 24th April 2011: Uterga
- 25th April 2011: Maneru
- 26th April 2011: Estella
- 27th April 2011: Los Arcos
- 28th April 2011: Viana

- 19th May 2011: Rabinal del Camino
- 20th May 2011: Acebo
- 21st May 2011: Ponferrada
- 22nd May 2011: Ponferrada
- 23rd May 2011: Villafranca del Bierzo
- 24th May 2011: Ruitelan
- 25th May 2011: O Cebreiro
- 26th May 2011: Triacastella
- 27th May 2011: San Mamed del Camino
- 28th May 2011: Portomarin
- 29th May 2011: Portos
- 30th May 2011: Palas de Rey
- 31st May 2011: Ribadiso
- 1st June 2011: Santa Irene
- 2nd June 2011: Santiago de Compostela
- 3rd June 2011: Santiago de Compostela

Acknowledgements

I would like to express my gratitude to:

1. My friend Roger Thiedeman, who gave so generously of his time, skills and experience to meticulously and expertly edit the manuscript for me.

2. Professor Christie Weeramantry for his wise observations and inspiring foreword.

3. Rohan Wijesekera and K.D. Ruwan Tharanga at Vijitha Yapa Publications for converting the manuscript and photographs into a publishable book.

4. Shivantha, who proved himself not only a good son but also a good friend. It is gratifying to realise that it is not just the colour of his hair and the shape of his nose that he has inherited from me – but also many of the values that I cherish.

5. Priyadarshini Menaka, my Spanish-speaking daughter, who ensured (even though I never came up to her exacting standards!) that I learned enough Spanish to make my way through Spain.

6. Chitra, who for over 35 years has been not only a wonderful wife and an excellent personal physician to me but has always given me good and (unforgettable!) advice.

7. The many folk – such as the optometrist in Carrion de Los Condes who fixed my glasses, the kind lady in Ventosa who bought us food when we were hungry, Ian and June from Devon who shared their meal with us in Navarette, and Greg from Canada who gave his warm winter coat to Shivantha in Logrono – whose innumerable kindnesses along the way eased our journey. These were recurrent reminders to us of the essential goodness of our fellow human beings – and that there is much more that unites us than divides us.

Foreword

This is a vivid description of a walk across Spain visiting Catholic religious shrines.

One of the primary world problems today is the lack of interest across religions. Cabinned, cribbed and confined within the faith to which they were born, the majority of people across the world remain in total unawareness of the richness of other faiths. This narrative is a valuable corrective to this trend.

Dr. Wijesinha's narrative shows one way in which we can generate more understanding across the religious divisions that artificially divide the world today. Dr. Wijesinha, although not himself a Catholic, has not only shown an interest in Catholic traditions and its saintly figures but has also undertaken with his son an 800 km walk visiting the sacred sites which Catholics revere in Northern Spain.

Strangers on the Camino reveals an insight not only into the lives of saintly figures involved but also their teaching and what they stood for. It contains much information unknown to the majority of Catholics themselves and shows the richness of these traditions as perceived by a non-Catholic. This is thus a lesson to people both Catholic and non-Catholic of the way in which inter-religious understanding can enrich our individual lives as well as our collective perception of the vast wealth of tradition and wisdom of world religions which lies largely untapped.

Through this narrative the reader also gains numerous insights into history, architecture, art, religious traditions, saintly lives and religious teachings of humility and service.

It is written very descriptively in the setting of a loving family relationship between a father and a son. They have had time to share each other's interests and enjoy each other's company in a manner which could stimulate other parents and children to minimise the distance that tends increasingly to separate parents and children in an age which makes so many claims upon their time.

I congratulate the author for having undertaken this trip and on having recorded it so meticulously. It should open the eyes of many to the potential there is for us all to learn much about other religions and their history.

C. G. Weeramantry
Former Vice President of the International Court of Justice

Weeramantry International Centre for Peace Education and Research, Colombo, April 2014

Chapter 1: In the Beginning

It was only when I was on the long SriLankan Airlines flight taking me on the first leg of my journey back home to Melbourne that I seriously contemplated the question that had long been nagging me.

Whatever had made me decide to walk the Camino de Santiago?

Sitting in the dark cabin of the aircraft with a plastic tumbler of Cognac on the tray table in front of me, and most of the other passengers fast asleep, I had the ideal opportunity, now that I had completed the journey, to contemplate the question. Whatever had made a conservative and unemotional man like me simply take six weeks off work and spend this time with his son hiking 800 kilometres across the north of Spain along an ancient pilgrim trail called the Camino de Santiago, when I had so many more 'important' things to do in my life: conduct a busy medical practice, teach medical students, write research papers and create wealth?

The Camino is not well known outside Europe. There, called The Way of Saint James in English, *Le Chemin de St Jacques* in French, *Jakobsweg* in German and *El Camino de Santiago* in Spanish, it has been attracting 'pilgrim' walkers for well over a thousand years.

Legend has it that the relics of Saint James, one of Jesus Christ's 12 apostles (called *Santiago* in Spanish) are buried in the magnificent cathedral of Santiago de Compostela in northwestern Spain. For centuries devout pilgrims, mostly Catholics, have been trekking their way from all over Europe to worship at the shrine.

I must confess that I am not a Catholic.

However, an oft-quoted 12th century poem reassured me that the Camino was '*open to all…the sick and the well, not only Catholics but also Jews, pagans, heretics and vagabonds.*'

Perhaps, I reasoned, since I have so many Jewish friends with whom I have shared *Shabbat* meals over the years, I could claim with credibility to be Jewish by adoption. On the other hand, since I belong to a traditional Buddhist family from Sri Lanka, I should be able to pass off as a rustic pagan. If all else fails, I reasoned that I might simply claim to be accepted as a heretic or a vagabond. But I need not have worried about my credentials. These days, around a hundred thousand 'pilgrims' walk or bicycle The Way each year – many for religious and spiritual reasons, others for cultural reasons, and yet others just for the physical challenge. In 1987 the Council of Europe designated the Camino as a 'Cultural Itinerary of Europe' – the first such route to be so honoured – and in 1993 UNESCO awarded it World Heritage status.

The number of Camino-walkers is rising, popularised perhaps by best-selling novels like Brazilian writer Paolo Coelho's *The Pilgrimage*, American movie star Shirley MacLaine's *The Camino – A Journey of the Spirit* and German TV personality Hape Kerkeling's *I'm Off Then.* No doubt *The Way* – Emilio Estevez's 2011 movie starring his father Martin Sheen as a father who walks the Camino in memory of his son who was killed soon after he set off to walk the Pilgrim Trail – will serve to attract even more pilgrims to undertake this journey.

The Camino consists of several trails originating in various parts of Europe that have been converging on Santiago since the

9th century when St James' tomb was first discovered there. The most popular is the *Via Frances*, or French Way, that commences in the little town of St Jean Pied de Port at the foothills of the Pyrenees in France, crosses the French-Spanish border and then traverses the length of northern Spain to reach the cathedral city (itself a World Heritage site) near the Atlantic coast. Five to seven weeks is the time most of those who undertake the Camino require to cover the 800 km path. Pilgrims however do not need to walk the whole way to benefit from the trek. Walking just the last hundred kilometres – or riding the last two hundred, either on horseback or bicycle – allows one to claim a *Compostela* (official Certificate of Completion) from the authorities at the cathedral in Santiago. We met folk who had set out to walk just part of the trail for a week or so – and others who, having walked a portion of The Way in the fortnight of annual leave they were allowed the previous year, had returned to continue their journey from where they had left off.

Recognising the contribution that so many thousand visitors make to their economies, the regional governments of Spain ensure that the path is clearly marked and well maintained. Every ten to fifteen kilometres there is convenient, cheap accommodation in the form of *albergues* run by local monasteries, municipalities and private individuals that, for around five or six Euros, offer pilgrims a place to sleep for the night. This is usually in dormitories with bunk beds, although a few do have a limited number of rooms available for about €20 per person. Some *albergues*, as well as most restaurants along the Camino, provide for about €10 a reasonable three-course pilgrim meal consisting of a soup or salad, a main dish of fish or meat, and a dessert – accompanied by water and/or wine. In order to avail oneself of the facilities at these *albergues*, one needs a Pilgrim Passport, known as a *Credencial*, which can be obtained from the pilgrim office in St Jean Pied de Port – or by post from one of the official Pilgrim Confraternities (e.g. American Pilgrims on the Camino http://www.americanpilgrims.com/).

And whether you do it for spiritual reasons, cultural reasons or just for the physical challenge, The Camino is certainly a path worth walking.

When was the last time, I asked myself, that I was able to step away from work matters – and do something that I wanted to do for myself? All we had to do on the Camino was walk at our own pace, stopping for the night or for a meal where fancy took us, even staying a day longer at places where we felt that we would like to see something of interest.

Perhaps it was the very simplicity of this idea that had attracted me in the first place: six weeks of travelling light, living out of a haversack and just – WALKING. It allowed me the opportunity of slackening the hectic pace of my life to the natural rhythm of human walking, dispensing with things like 'to do' lists, work schedules and palm pilot planners.

What better way to spend a glorious spring day than hiking through beautiful country in the company of my son, admiring picturesque views of the Pyrenees or passing through quaint Spanish villages that still retain a medieval air? We crossed Roman bridges over 2,000 years old, passed through ancient walled towns like Astorga, and walked past impressive Templar castles such as the one at Ponferrada. When we reached the big cities, we often took a day off to see the tourist sights in the vicinity – such as the amazing new Museum of Human Evolution in Burgos or the magnificent Cathedral in Leon. At the end of the day's walk we had the choice of staying in a cheap *albergue* or a less inexpensive *pensione* or motel.

Sitting in the darkened airplane cabin I took another sip of Cognac, closed my eyes and took my mind back to the people, places and events that would forever remain with me as my memories of the Camino.

I smiled to myself as I remembered Roland who had left his farm in Lyons in France to walk all the way to Santiago with his pet donkey Praline. My mind lingered wistfully on the image of the picturesque river at Logrono, beside which we had a picnic lunch with Greg who, having walked with us during his two weeks of annual leave, was leaving that evening to return to Canada - and I recalled with a deep sense of contentment the evening we spent at the Albergue San Nicolas, a restored 12th century hospice where we had our evening meal by candlelight and then sat outside with our *companeros* to watch the sunset.

If you decide to walk the Camino yourself, you can walk alone (which gives time for reflection), undertake the journey with a friend or family member (as I did with my son) or use the opportunity to meet people and make new friends.

Was my desire to undertake this journey due to an interest in ancient history and contemporary Spain - or a search for something spiritual - or simply the result of a personal quest and the desire to prove to myself that, at the age when most of my colleagues have retired from their lifelong jobs, I could still accomplish a challenge like this?

Was it a desire to spend time with my son, getting to know him as an adult and a colleague?

Having walked the entire 800 km and had plenty of time to reflect on my experience, I am still not sure what made me decide to do it.

But I am certainly glad that I made my decision – and did it.

Chapter 2: What, When and How

What?

Looking back now that I have completed the journey, I cannot recall when it was that I first discovered that there was an entity called the Camino de Santiago.

It may have been a magazine article – or perhaps something I heard on the radio or even a TV programme I saw – which made me aware of the existence of the pilgrim trail to Santiago de Compostela. It may have had something to do with my son enjoying Paolo Coelho's book *The Pilgrimage* so much that he gave me a copy for my birthday, and talked of the possibility of someday walking the Camino himself.

"*Tha*," he said to me one day, using the diminutive Sinhalese word for Father (*Thaththa*) that he had been calling me from the time he first learned to talk, "maybe one day we can walk the Camino together, just you and me."

Gradually, almost imperceptibly, *El Camino* became something I thought about frequently – and read about at every opportunity. Over the past few years this idea of a pilgrimage grew into something I felt that I would like to undertake. I have realised that in life we have no idea how much time we have left – so it's best not to waste any of it. If you decide that something is worth doing, then you should go ahead and get on with doing it.

I often think of my friend Derek, a busy and successful surgeon who for many years used to visit our clinic every

Thursday afternoon to see patients. One evening, shortly before he retired, we had both finished seeing our patients earlier than we expected, so we poured ourselves cups of tea and sat chatting in his consulting room – a rare occurrence, because he was always rushing off after he finished consultations to some hospital where he had a patient booked in for operation. He told me enthusiastically that day of his plans to go on a long trip to Europe the following year with his wife – something they had wanted to do for many years but had put off until he reached the age of 65 and was able to retire from the staff of our large public hospital. Derek's wife had just obtained the appropriate brochures from the travel agent and had borrowed the relevant Lonely Planet, Insight and Footprint books from the library – and they were eagerly looking forward to spending three months the following summer travelling through England, France, Italy and Germany.

I will never forget that evening with him.

The next time I saw Derek was in hospital two months later – where he was a patient after having been diagnosed with metastatic pancreatic cancer. The disease had silently spread throughout his body while he was busy working as a surgeon – and by the time it was discovered neither surgery nor chemotherapy could control it. Derek died six months to the day that we had our Thursday evening conversation about his planned post-retirement holiday – a holiday that he never got the chance to take because he was so busy working.

The shrine at Santiago de Compostela – the capital city of Galicia, one of the autonomous regions of northern Spain – is reputed to be the burial place of St James, who was not only one of Jesus' 12 apostles but also the son of his mother Mary's own sister Salome. After the death of Jesus, legend has it that St James (*SanTiago* in Spanish) travelled to Galicia and spent a number of years preaching there before returning to Jerusalem where he was martyred by being beheaded. His followers are believed to have brought his headless body back to Spain, and the place where his remains are said to have been buried (*Compostela* means 'The Field of Stars' in Spanish) became a site of veneration and homage. In 1175, Pope Alexander III designated Santiago de Compostela a holy city worthy of pilgrimage, as were Rome and Jerusalem. It soon became one of the major destinations of pilgrimage authorised by the Roman Catholic church. Even today it remains one of the most visited shrines in Christendom.

Now Jerusalem is the city that is most closely associated with the life of Jesus Christ, and Rome is the centre of the church's political power and the resting place of both St Peter and St Paul. A Christian undertaking a long journey to worship at either of these places could certainly justify the effort and expenditure as a worthy undertaking, similar to a Moslem making the holy *Hajj* pilgrimage to Mecca or a Buddhist going on pilgrimage to the site of the Buddha's enlightenment in Bodhgaya.

But Santiago on the other hand had little to make it attractive to prospective pilgrims except the simple idea of a long walk, a trek that led to the tomb of neither Jesus Christ himself nor even his chief disciple Peter. All that one found at the end were the relics of the lesser of Jesus' cousins, James, a man who had done precious little to distinguish himself in life – a disciple who preached little, wrote less and died young.

During the Middle Ages however Santiago de Compostela became arguably the most famous goal of pilgrimage in Europe – and in recent years the city has enjoyed a remarkable revival of that role with a few hundred footsore pilgrims streaming each day into the cathedral in Santiago to attend the daily pilgrims' service.

Although some of my good friends are Catholics and I have great respect for the Christian religion and the Catholic faith, I cannot label myself as being a member of any particular religious group. Exposure in childhood to saintly grandmothers on either side of my family, each of whom belonged to a different religion, has left me with a great respect for ALL spiritual beliefs – and a healthy cynicism or (perhaps even a distrust of) all forms of organised and institutionalised religion. I firmly believe that one can love and appreciate the game of soccer without becoming a soccer hooligan or blindly swearing allegiance to either the Glasgow Rangers or Glasgow Celtic Club. When it comes to fostering goodwill on earth and peace among men, the purveyors of institutionalised religion have been as helpful in promoting love and harmony as cricketers who verbally abuse their opponents (the act is euphemistically termed 'sledging') on the sports field and then claim that they love and promote the game of cricket.

However, as I seriously thought about undertaking this journey myself, I was reassured by another version of that 12th century poem I had read:

'Its doors are open to all – well and ill, Catholics but also Jews, pagans, and heretics, the idler and the vagabond – and to put it shortly, the good and the wicked.'

I could comfortably see myself fitting into at least two of those categories – and thus reassured that even this Sri Lankan-born Australian would make an acceptable pilgrim, I decided that I too would undertake this journey traversing the long, arduous and not always picturesque routes across the cold mountains and hot *mesetas* of Spain. It would not be a religious pilgrimage but a physical, perhaps even a spiritual, pilgrimage.

When?

The decision having been made to undertake the pilgrimage, the question was when I should do it. If I kept putting it off much more, I told myself, I might soon be too old or too unhealthy to make the journey. In 2011 I would be eligible for a spell of sabbatical leave from my job as an associate professor at Monash University, Melbourne, and because my son Shivantha would finally be finishing his studies in North America in February of that year, I suggested to him that we undertake the walk together – the period between him being a full-time student and commencing employment, the period when he would be getting off my payroll and (hopefully) at last putting all his university education into gainful employment to earn his daily bread.

This book is neither a diary of my travels (although the diary I kept during my long walk to Santiago has helped me to recall impressions I formed and the information I acquired along the way), nor is it a guidebook for travellers along the road to Santiago (although it will probably be of benefit to others like me who might be contemplating undertaking the walk themselves). It may be of interest to armchair travellers who, from the comfort of their own homes, might like to read about unusual journeys and strange places.

Primarily, this book is a personal account: what it was like for a three-score-year-old doctor and his not-so-old son to spend 45 days walking 20- to 30,000 paces each day, lugging our 15 kilogram backpacks for 800 km along the ancient pilgrim route, staying in *albergues por los peregrinos* (pilgrim hostels) – and experiencing at first-hand what it is like to be 21st century pilgrims. It is a tale of our discoveries: about the land we traversed, the journey we undertook, the people we met, the father and son who started this journey – and the two friends who completed it.

How?

Having made the decision to undertake the long walk to Santiago, it was time to prepare. I am a firm believer in the saying 'Proper Preparation Prevents Poor Performance' – which had been dinned into us *ad nauseam* throughout our schooldays. If memory serves me right, I first heard the phrase from my old scoutmaster Wilson Muttiah when he gently chided me after a particularly badly organised scout camp for which I was responsible.

And I could almost hear my dear friend Rakki Jayawardena, as he recounted to me the story of how he had accomplished yet another of his many successful business ventures, repeating his famous words of advice: "'Sanjo', if ever you fail to plan, you are planning to fail."

So I decided to Plan – and to Prepare Properly for my adventure.

But where should I start?

As a first step I went to the local libraries in Melbourne and searched on their shelves and computers for any books about the Camino. I was lucky to locate in the Albury public library a delightful book entitled *Pray for me in Santiago* by Theresa Burkhardt-Fuller, a Swiss lady living in Perth at the time, who together with her husband Gerard walked the Camino Frances when they were both in their sixties.

The book had so much useful information and proved so inspiring that I wrote to Mrs Burkhardt-Fuller to tell her how much I had enjoyed the book and that I was planning to undertake the journey the following year. I received an encouraging reply from her.

Many years ago, when I was up at Oxford undertaking the research project that was to lead to my postgraduate degree, I discovered after I had finally decided on the subject of my research, what a wealth of information was available about the topic. When I mentioned this fact to my teacher, Dr Malcolm Gough, he smilingly informed me that once you develop an interest in a topic, you become sensitised to information about it. Almost as if by serendipity you are then drawn to various items connected with your new interest – items that were always there, perhaps, but which you were not sensitised to notice.

Paolo Coelho expressed something similar when he wrote in his book *The Alchemist*, 'And when you want something, all the universe conspires in helping you to achieve it.'

Now help from the Universe and others, while always welcome, is not enough without careful preparation – and I have to admit that we would not have been able to successfully complete our Camino if we had not prepared carefully.

Hardly anyone we met walking the Camino was free of foot, ankle or knee problems. Blisters were a common sight – as were *peregrinos* limping along the trail or spending long periods in the *albergues* massaging their feet. Observing so many with these blisters, knee problems, back problems etc, I was initially surprised as to why I was relatively free of these ailments until Shivantha pointed out to me, "*Tha*, don't forget that you trained – and dealt with your blisters and foot problems during your early training while you were at home BEFORE you set off for France."

This could certainly explain the matter. For about a year before I left for France, I had been walking regularly – for at least an hour three times a week either on the walking track called the Koonung Creek Trail near our home or on the treadmill at our local gym. As the time for our Camino grew closer, I started wearing my hiking boots for these walks –and in January (three months before our start date) I bought myself a new pair of hiking boots. The first couple of days when I hiked in these new boots, I developed blisters on my heels, so I stayed off the boots until the blisters healed – and once the skin over the healed blisters had hardened, I started wearing these boots to walk again. There were no further blisters.

Another tip I had learned was to wear two pairs of thick cotton socks and to wash them out thoroughly at the end of the day. Socks absorb a tremendous amount of sweat during a walking day, and this can predispose to fungal infections. Put on two pairs of dry socks each morning – and the socks that were washed the previous night, if not yet dry, could be strung on one's backpack to dry during the day.

My training was not limited to one-hour walks on the treadmill. On several Saturdays, I set off on walks of three to four hours' duration – gradually building up endurance and training myself to keep well hydrated. By the time I was ready to leave for France, I had done several four-hour walks carrying my backpack – along the Koonung Creek Trail from Bulleen Road to Springvale Road and back, from our home to Hoddle Street in the city, on a circuit around the town of Morwell – and even up the 'Thousand Steps' trail in the Dandenongs.

Having prepared so intensively even before I stepped out of St Jean Pied de Port, I hadn't the heart to make any helpful comments to those fellow pilgrims who unpacked their brand-new sneakers and, cigarettes dangling from their lips, started lacing up their new unbroken shoes prior to setting off on the trail.

How else did I prepare for my trek?

About two years before we actually set off, I enrolled at the local adult education centre for Spanish lessons. This was partly due to the influence of my daughter, who had developed a love for the language and has recently completed a postgraduate diploma in Spanish language. The three hours I spent each Wednesday for four semesters left me with, if not a fluent knowledge of the language, at least enough Spanish to find my way along the Camino.

My little knowledge of Spanish made me mortally scared to fall sick in Spain, since the Spanish words for health and medical matters often mean something quite different to what English-speakers think they mean. *Constipacion* for example means not its equivalent in English, but 'common cold' – while *embarrasada* means not 'embarrassed' but 'pregnant'. I had nightmares of myself presenting at a clinic in Spain and stating, "I am embarrassed that I have a cold"; and the nurse understanding me to be saying, "I am pregnant because I am constipated"!

In order to avoid any contact with the Spanish health care system except for the most life-threatening conditions, we took along an adequate first aid kit – my usual medications, paracetamol, oral rehydration salts, bandaids and chemical hot packs. Better to be well prepared and not require any of this than undertake the Camino with no medical supplies at all. It goes without saying that taking adequate health insurance for the duration of the Camino was a pre-requisite of our going.

And most important, the pilgrim who wants to walk the Camino must accept the fact that he has to travel light. Pack no more than ten kilograms in your backpack (a useful rule of thumb is to carry a backpack no heavier than a tenth of your body weight) and leave behind all but the most essential items.

Plate 1

1A: The Father

1B: The Son

1C: The Holy Trail

Plate 2

2A: Friends of the Camino: Jasek, the Pole in the Rain

2B: Friends of the Camino – Roland with his donkey Praline

Plate 3

3A: Friends of the Camino – Farewell to Greg

3B: Friends of the Camino – Coffee with Ruggero

Plate 4

4A: Music on the Camino - Shivantha and his harmonica

4B: Music on the Camino – Jam session at San Mamed del Camino

Chapter 3: Leaving Home

Thursday 14th April & Friday 15th April 2011: Colombo to Paris

Sri Lanka's traditional New Year dawned this year on April 14th – the beginning of a new year and an auspicious start to my journey. Having checked in for my flight on the internet, I was collected at 11.30 pm by an Airport Express taxi and taken to Katunayake International Airport to board SriLankan Airlines flight 563 to Paris.

After clearing immigration with my three polythene-wrapped bags (packed haversack, sleeping bag and a red, blue and white plastic bag containing my boots and walking clothes) I walked up to the Vijitha Yapa airport bookshop and was browsing as is my usual habit, when I heard an announcement for me to report to Gate 15 as the flight was starting to board. It would certainly have been disastrous if after all my planning I missed my flight (as had happened to me once before at Sydney airport).

I was fortunate to be allocated a seat with the one next to me vacant – with the result that I was able to stretch out, read, write postcards, watch TV and sleep in comfort through most of the flight.

I arrived at Charles de Gaulle airport around 10 am on April 15th, and after collecting my three bags I was amazed at how quickly I came through immigration control. The officer just glanced at my Australian passport and stamped it, without even asking for how long I would be staying.

I was directed by the lady at Information to take the IntraTrain to Hall 5 in Terminal 3, from where I got the shuttle bus to Hotel Millenium in the Village Roissy near the airport. The driver of the shuttle bus was a tall dark African who was in obvious good spirits and talking animatedly with his off-duty colleague. I managed to join in their conversation in my limited French, and allowed them to share with me the good news that they had just won money on the horses!

With time to spare I relaxed with a swim in the hotel pool and then sat in the hotel's Jules Verne bar with a glass of rosé wine, just sitting and savouring the pleasure of actually being here. Sitting doing nothing is not something I am used to. My friend Gamani once told me that I am someone who always needs to be doing something active – he could not ever imagine me sitting and "just being" because I have given him the impression that I consider relaxation a waste of time.

Well, the start of my Camino would be a good time to start changing.

While I was swimming in the warm pool, I saw the bright sunlight in the courtyard outside – and my immediate reaction was to think, "I must finish my swim quickly so I can go out there and enjoy a glass of wine in the sunshine."

And then realisation dawned. I said to myself: "What is this foolishness? Instead of enjoying the swim, here I am thinking that I must curtail it to do something else that appears at this moment to be better – and I am almost certain, when sitting out in the sun with my glass of wine, to be making plans (rather than enjoying the moment) to go and do something else from there!"

I reflected that walking the Camino would teach me some useful lessons for life – and what I had just realised was a good beginning to what I would later come to call my list of 'Camino Lessons'.

So this was Camino Lesson Number 1: ***Live in the moment. Enjoy what you have the good fortune to be doing. Don't spend every moment of the present planning how to achieve some future pleasure – just enjoy the pleasure of the present.***

I had a while to wait until my son arrived, so I went back to my room and slept until around 8.30. I then came down to the lobby and sat in a comfortable chair from where I had a good view of the hotel entrance, and was seated there when Shivantha walked in and went up to the reception desk. He did not recognise me at first because I was almost bald, having taken a 'Number Nought' haircut the previous day in Colombo! With him studying in New York and me being in Melbourne we had not seen each other for about ten months.

After we had shared a huge bear hug, we went up to our room where he deposited his baggage in our room and freshened up. We then walked down to Roissy village and had dinner. I ordered *Noix de St Jacques* – loosely and irreverently translated it means 'The Nuts of St James' – which turned out to be deliciously prepared scallops. At the hotel which had Wi-Fi we were able to talk to my wife Chitra and his girlfriend Irma on Skype. Shivantha had brought his laptop in his haversack and planned to carry it with him on the Camino. His justification for the extra weight was that this would allow him to keep in touch with his mother and report how father and son were doing – but I suspect the real reason was so he could talk every day to his girlfriend in Italy.

He explained to me – an avowed technophobe – about Skype and Wi-Fi. Apparently most hotels and establishments (Starbucks in the USA is a prime example) provide free access to the internet for their clients. Unlike him, I am averse to embracing new-fangled gadgets. Surprising though it may sound, I have thus far resisted even the idea of carrying a mobile phone.

How the world has changed in my own short lifetime. To think that just a few hundred years ago, pilgrims leaving to walk the Camino would be out of touch with their loved ones at home for the entire period of their pilgrimage!

Saturday 16th & Sunday 17th April 2011: Paris to St Jean Pied de Port

The following morning we enjoyed the buffet breakfast in the Millenium Hotel, and while Shivantha got on his computer, I went for a walk to Roissy Village – a charming wooded oasis in the vicinity of Charles de Gaulle airport. Once upon a time it was a farming village with a chateau, and in the village there were pictures from the last century, showing scenes of Roissy at a time when 'life ran its unerring course humbly, in the healthy rural routine of harsh physical labour'. Life in those days was short and uncertain. How many of the folk in these black-and-white pictures had lived to what we in the 21st century deem 'old age'?

Very few, I suspect, would have made it past 60 – and here I was presuming to embark on the Camino at 60.

I recall some months ago using the words "Being born into this world is a death sentence" when talking with Carol, one of my patients who had just been diagnosed with advanced liver cancer. She had been my patient for many years, and our relationship had developed from being simply doctor and patient to being two old friends – so much so that her visits to see me at the clinic were enjoyable conversations rather than formal consultations. We discussed that day the idea that all of us are on this earth for a finite time, and none of knows how much time we will be allowed to spend here. One benefit of discovering that you have a terminal illness is that you become aware that your days are limited – and so you can take steps to do the things you had always wanted to do instead of putting them off because "I just don't have the time for it at the moment." I remember Carol telling me with a smile as she and her husband left my room that day, "Doctor, what I have realised is that Life itself is a terminal illness – and in my case I am lucky because unlike most people, I have a good idea of how much time I have left."

Life then is a journey between the time we are born and the time we die. None of us knows how long our journey will last. For some of us the journey is short, for others long – but whatever the length of the journey it is better to enjoy one's journey and make the best of one's travel time instead of waiting impatiently or with resignation for the destination to be reached. I felt thankful that morning in Roissy to be alive – and healthy enough to avail myself of this opportunity to walk the Camino with my son.

We checked out of the hotel at noon and got the shuttle bus to the Charles De Gaulle train station, where we waited for the TGV train to Bordeaux. Reaching Bordeaux around nine in the evening we walked over to the Hotel Ibis where we had dinner and slept.

The following morning I was up as usual at 6 am – I have always been an early riser. Thanks to my son's laptop (for which I was to become increasingly grateful as our journey progressed) I was able to send emails to my wife and daughter as well as several friends around the world. After he woke, we went down to have breakfast: coffee, cereal, croissants, crepes, tortillas, yoghurt and fruit, as well as a couple of local specialties.

By 9.30 we were able to leave for the Bordeaux St Jean station to take the train to Bayonne. Here we had a couple of hours to wait for our train to St Jean Pied de Port. Crossing the bridge over the river Nive, we walked to the imposing and elegant Gothic Cathedral, *La Cathédrale Sainte-Marie*. The famed cloisters were closed, but we were able to admire them through the windows. Having had a bite to eat in a small restaurant in the plaza, we walked back to the station to get the slow SNCF train to St Jean Pied de Port, which would be the starting point for our long walk to Santiago.

Waiting for the train we were intrigued to realise that there were quite a few others like us, all carrying backpacks with scallop shells around their necks or pinned to their backpacks. These shells are considered to be the symbol of St James, and those walking the Camino usually have such a shell to identify themselves as pilgrims. We realised that we were not alone. At last, here were fellow pilgrims!

How many of these shell-bedecked, backpack-laden folk were setting out to walk the 800 km to Santiago in order to pray at the shrine of St James? Which among them were here to hike the ancient tracks that would take them through rural Spain and give them the chance of enjoying the food and wine of this region – and which were the fitness freaks who would be trying to get there in the fastest possible time? Some had national flags sewn on to their caps or backpacks; there were many Scandinavians and Americans identifying themselves thus, as well as a couple of Canadians who proudly displayed on their kit both the Canadian flag (to avoid, I presumed, the ignominy of being mistaken for Americans) as well as the distinctive flag of Quebec (to ensure they would not be mistaken for Anglo-Canadians).

The train passed through some lovely scenery, skirting a river with woods, white houses, meadows and sheep. We arrived in St Jean Pied de Port in the afternoon and walked to the Hotel Remparts for which I had taken the precaution of making a reservation previously. We changed and went for a walk in the town – passing the Port d'Espagne (the gateway through which pilgrims passed through on their way to Spain), the old Roman bridge and *L'eglise Notre Dame du Bout de Pont* (The Church of Our Lady at the Foot of the Bridge).

We were standing at the closed door of this 14th century church looking at the notice giving the times of church services, when the door opened from inside and a lady came out. We asked her about services and although she was just closing up for the evening she kindly offered to let us in and wait while we had a look inside the church. We humbly entered, our voices lowering to whispers as we walked around, admiring the statues and paintings within. Why is it that we always speak in whispers when inside these small places of worship, even if there are no others inside? Is it that we sense the presence of those whom we cannot see?

We stopped in front of the altar and lit a candle to mark the commencement of our journey, remembering our family in Melbourne, my father in Colombo and especially my mother who had passed away in 1997. It was she who had looked after Shivantha while my wife and I were overseas studying, and of all her grandchildren she always had a special fondness for him.

We left the church after graciously thanking the lady for her kindness.

Shivantha and I found a pleasant restaurant close to the church – Restaurant Oillarburu – for our evening meal. Wanting to conform to my usual vegetarian diet I ordered a vegetable soup (*Gerbure*) which I soon discovered contained several tasty chunks of ham. In fact it had more pieces of ham than pieces of vegetable in it. As we shared a bottle of *Axeridoy*, a wine typical of the Basque country, I told Shivantha that on this journey I would have to be flexible with regard to my food – justifying this with the rationalisation that after four hours of walking every day it would not really matter how much sugar or fat I ate, because my physical exercise would burn it all up. The *Gerbure* was followed by scrambled eggs and ham, and for dessert we sampled the local specialty of goat's cheese and berry jam.

Monday 18th April 2011: St Jean Pied de Port

Waking up at six as usual, I let my son sleep while I washed my clothes and hung them out on the balcony to dry. After this I went for a walk up to the Citadelle, from where I had a great view of St Jean and its surroundings. Returning around eight I woke him to have breakfast. We had agreed previously that today would be a rest day for us – a day to gather our strength for the journey ahead.

For many years, pilgrims traveling along the Camino have been able to obtain an official document of identification, a Pilgrim Passport called a *Credencial,* which identifies them as pilgrims and allows them to avail themselves of the very reasonably priced special accommodation along the way. In years gone by, many of these pilgrim hostels (called *aubergues* or *gites* in France and *albergues* or *refugios* in Spain) were maintained by local churches, religious organisations and various confraternities. All a pilgrim had to do in return for accommodation (and sometimes even a communal meal) was to leave a small donation when he or she left in the morning. These days, most *refugios* along the Camino charge a small fee from pilgrims – of the order of five to eight Euros, with sometimes a simple meal on offer for another eight to 12 Euros.

At every *refugio* as well as at various restaurants, churches and similar establishments on the way, pilgrims can have their *Credencials* officially stamped (the rubber stamp is called a *sello*) with the date and details of the place. At the end of the pilgrim's journey, the *Credencial* with its series of *sellos* could be presented to the Cathedral Office in Santiago de Compostela as evidence that he or she has actually walked the Camino – and this entitles the pilgrim to receive the official certificate of completion called a *Compostela.*

After breakfast we walked to the pilgrim office Accueil on the Rue de Citadelle where we got the first *sello* in our *Credencials*

– and our first taste of the help and advice that pilgrims are privileged to receive on the Camino. Following our meeting with the very helpful staff at the Accueil who gave us advice about the route we could follow and the weather we could expect, I went up to the Citadelle again - this time with Shivantha.

We then visited the local post office to send off postcards, bought some food from the local supermarket and then strolled over to the river bank where we sat near the old Roman stone bridge beneath some leafy old trees and had a picnic lunch – sardines, asparagus, strawberries and a bottle of St Emilion wine. It had been a long time since father and son had been able to sit on a grassy bank in the company of a gently flowing river on a peaceful spring afternoon and share a meal, conversation and glass of wine – with Time put on hold and no deadlines to meet.

After a very pleasant couple of hours we returned to the hotel and sat out in the sun on the balcony, reading and planning our journey for the morrow.

Dinner was at the same restaurant near the church. Once more I had their Gerbure (which we decided would better be described on the menu as ham soup rather than vegetable soup). For dessert we sampled another local specialty, the Gateaux Basque.

Chapter 4: A Journey of a Thousand Miles

Tuesday 19th April 2011: St Jean Pied de Port to Orisson

The day on which we would commence our walk dawned clear, auguring well for our journey. We had our coffee and croissants and left the Hotel Remparts at 7.15 am, passing through the Porte D'Espagne to commence our journey along the Route Napoleon – the route along which in 1808 Napoleon Bonaparte led his troops on their conquest of Spain. The route however is much older than Napoleon, being part of the Roman Via Traiana that extended from Burdigala (Bordeaux) to Asturica Augusta (Astorga).

The path gradually climbed uphill, so I took it slowly with regular stops. Shivantha's pack at 17 kg was much heavier than it should have been. In addition to his pack he was carrying the bag of food we had purchased at the local supermarket, while I had in my hand the small black bag containing camera, passports and books that I usually take as my hand luggage when travelling by plane. After about three hours of climbing we came upon Madame Ourthiague's place in Huntto and stopped for a coffee and rest. Here we sat with Helle, a fellow pilgrim from Denmark who works as a nurse in a psychiatric clinic. While the three of us were seated together at a table for four, sipping our coffee, we saw a young man coming down the path, heading towards St Jean Pied de Port. "Hey, you are going the wrong way!" Helle shouted to him in the voice that I am sure she uses on errant patients. He stopped in his tracks and looked in our direction, somewhat perplexed at this perfect stranger addressing him so authoritatively – so I waved and suggested he join us for a coffee.

And this is how we met Fadi Feria -- born in Italy to parents from Lebanon, working in France and fluent in four languages – who came to be one of our closest companions on the Camino. As he told us later, he was coming down the mountain because he had decided that the Camino was too much for him, and he was on his way down to take the train back to Paris.

Fadi and Shivantha got chatting over coffee, and soon found they had a lot in common. When we stood up to go we suggested he walk up with us – and this chance meeting with us, according to Fadi, was what made him change his mind and continue on the Camino.

Walking through the Pyrenees along this stretch of the Camino – probably one of the most physically demanding sectors of The Way – we were treated to amazing views of the magnificent natural landscape, the great panorama of the Pyrenees. We saw Griffon vultures soaring in the mountain air currents, as well as the black-faced Manech sheep that provide the milk from which the local specialty Ossan Iraty cheese is made.

Around noon we stopped for lunch (cheese, figs, chocolate croissants and water that we had carried with us from St Jean) at a grassy spot from where, looking behind us, we had a clear view of the difficult path up the mountain that we had travelled. It gave us confidence to tackle the uphill path ahead of us.

At about 1 pm we reached the Orisson Auberge, our first *refugio* on the Camino. We sat ourselves down at a table outside with a great view of the surrounding mountains, and enjoyed a bottle of Axeridoy wine with Fadi and Helle.

I had prudently booked accommodation here before I left Australia. Shivantha and I were given the upper and lower bunks of a double bunk bed, in a room that had three more similar bunk beds. It was designed to accommodate eight people, and reminded me of the time I worked in Hong Kong where most apartments were tiny. In those Hong Kong flats, a bedroom meant just that – a space that had room for a bed or two, and little else. Fortunately the only time that all eight of the occupants were in the room at the same time was when we were sleeping.

Toilets and showers with hot water were outside; a communal dinner was provided in the large dining room downstairs – the ubiquitous *Gerbure*, pork with white beans, *Gateaux Basque* and the house red wine. After dinner the 30 or so of us had to get up and introduce ourselves, a good icebreaker even though the introductions were made in either English, French or Spanish. I made halting dinner table conversation in my limited French with a lady next to me who spoke equally limited English. After she and her husband had got up at the end of the meal, I turned to a lady who was now seated two places away from me and asked her, speaking very slowly, enunciating each word deliberately and carefully, "May I speak with you in English?" She laughed and replied in a broad Queensland accent, "Please do, I don't speak anything else!" And so acquaintance was made with Leonie Davies from Brisbane, who was planning to walk the entire Camino together with her daughter Claire, just as Shivantha and I were planning to do.

While I was conversing in Australian 'Strine' with Leonie, Shivantha had got into conversation with Claire and also Gregoire Crevier from Canada. It was a pleasant evening, sharing the meal and conversation with fellow pilgrims who like us had set out to undertake this same long walk to Santiago.

Wednesday 20th April 2011: Orisson to Roncesvalles

I was up at five the following morning, and after a visit to the cold toilet went out to watch the sunrise over the mountains. It was that time of day when one's mind is particularly lucid, when the unlimited visibility allows one, as dawn breaks and light gradually suffuses the landscape, to notice distant details. Beautiful!

After a breakfast of milk coffee (French style, in a bowl) followed by bread, butter and jam, we left Auberge Orisson around eight. Our plan, after covering 8 km on our first day, was to walk the 17 km to Roncesvalles by afternoon on this our second day.

This sector, similar to yesterday's journey, was tough going. The wind in these mountains is cold and fierce. We saw skeletons of sheep that had been picked clean by vultures. I was well aware that at my age over-enthusiastic physical exertion in the cold could precipitate an attack of angina, so we had planned to take the journey slowly. Our objective was not to get to our destination as fast as we could, ahead of everybody else – but simply to reach our destination safely.

I took one small step after the other, and Shivantha, conscious of the fact that his father was almost twice his age, kept pace with me. Would my ego be happy accepting this reversal in our roles – the son keeping a watchful eye out in case his father needed assistance? I have seen so many of my patients, as they get older and more frail, finding it difficult to accept the fact that they can no longer do what they were able to easily do 40 years ago, and now need the care of their children. Fear of losing their independence and becoming reliant on their offspring prevents them from accepting the help which their children are happy to give them – which would make life so much easier for them.

Would I be able to let go of my pride and allow myself to accept assistance when I needed it? Only Time would tell.

About half an hour after we had left the Auberge Orisson, we looked back and downwards along the path we had just travelled. How small the *auberge* looked in the distance. Yesterday on the other hand, when we were striving to reach it after our tough climb from St Jean and eagerly anticipating achieving our goal, it appeared so large as we rounded the last bend and came upon it. Today, we had another goal to achieve, the Abbey at Roncesvalles - and yesterday's much-awaited goal and major achievement now appeared so small.

After a while we reached the 1,100 metre-high Pic D'Orisson, with its image of the Virgin of Orisson set against an impressive backdrop of the surrounding mountains. Proceeding, we reached the border crossing between France and Spain, the milestone somewhat of an anti-climax because there was just a cattle grid to mark the spot, and a stone marker informing us that we were no longer in France but now in the Spanish province of Navarra.

About 4 km later we reached the Col de Lepoeder, at 1,400 metres the highest point of our journey through the Pyrenees. From here we descended through a lovely beech forest to reach the Abbey and Albergue of Roncesvalles by 3 pm – a total of just under seven hours' walking for the day. Even at the slow pace at which I had tackled the uphill stretches of the climb through the Pyrenees, we had reached our destination well in time and with no mishaps!

This, I reflected, was my second Camino Lesson: ***No enterprise is too difficult to accomplish as long as you take it slowly. Take one small step after another and constantly keep your main objective in sight.***

The Roncesvalles Albergue is well organised. Shivantha helped translate the Dutch *hospitalero*'s English into Italian for one man – who returned the favour by agreeing to exchange his allocated bunk with me so Shivantha and I could have bunks one above the other. I had a hot shower, after which my son gave me a massage for my aching trapezius and rhomboid muscles. I rested in my bunk for a while before we went for the communal pilgrim dinner (pasta, fish and chips, yoghurt and wine) and then attended the pilgrim mass in the Abbey, where the priest welcomed the *peregrinos* from various countries that he named. We were quite pleased to hear him acknowledge the "pilgrims from Sri Lanka" as well!

I tested my blood sugar – which after the long walk was down to 3.8 – proof, if I needed it, that aggressive physical exercise is the best therapy for keeping blood sugar under control in diabetes. Internet access was available here for €1.50 for half an hour, so we sent email messages to Chitra and my daughter Menaka in Melbourne, and my sister Anila in Colombo – and I was able to check my bank account to make sure I had received the refund for my overpayment from SNCF railways. I was beginning to realise the value of 21st century technology and staying connected. Perhaps by the end of the journey I will have overcome my fear of carrying a mobile phone that would make me over-contactable and over-connected.

Chapter 5: Navarra and the Basque Country

Thursday 21st April 2011: Roncesvalles to Zubiri

It was cold during the night – so cold that I had to use my sleeping bag as a blanket. We woke up early and were ready to leave by 7 am. When I was putting on my boots in the foyer downstairs, I discovered that we did not have my camera. We made a careful search through both Shivantha's and my pockets and bags – as well as in the cupboards and under the bunks in the cubicle in which we slept – but it proved futile. We even went back to the Sabina bar, where we had gone for a coffee after the pilgrim mass, but the camera, which had about a hundred pictures taken between Paris and Roncesvalles, including those taken during our walk through the Pyrenees, was gone.

There was no way we could find the camera. I had to accept the loss and move forward.

As we walked away from the *albergue* we worked out what must have happened. After the pilgrims' mass the previous night we had gone to the crowded bar with a group – Fadi, Helle, Leonie, Claire and Greg – to have a drink. I sat at a small table with the others while Fadi and Shivantha went up to the bar to get us our drinks. While Shivantha used both his hands to bring the two cups (my coffee and his hot chocolate) to our table, he had left the camera along with his diary on the bar table – and when he went back to get them, he had taken the diary, not realising at the time that the camera was missing. Somebody standing at

Plate 5

5A: Metal Sculpture at the Alto de Perdon

5B: Bridge at Puenta La Reina

Plate 6

6A: Church at Eunate

6B: Frescoes at Villatuerta Church

Plate 7

7A: Cathedral at Burgos

7B: Cathedral at Leon

Plate 8

8A: Castle at Ponferrada

8B: Monastery at Samos

the bar would have seen the camera – a Canon Powershot worth about 300 Australian dollars – and pocketed it.

Camino Lesson Number Three: ***Not everyone who comes on the Camino comes here with good intentions. Remember the old saying: 'Trust in God – but make sure to tether your camel'.***

Leaving the *albergue*, we walked with Fadi through a leafy wood outside Roncesvalles called the Witches' Forest (was this a place where in years gone by, wise women who the Church and State felt threatened by, were burned at the stake?) to the village of Burguete where we stopped for breakfast at the Café Fronton. From there we walked on through Espinal and Viskarret, ancient Basque hamlets that have probably been catering to pilgrims for the past few hundred years. We bought some food – cheese, chorizo, tinned seafood and wine – from the shop just outside Viskarret, and having walked through dense woodland, stopped for lunch in a clearing by our path between Linzoain and Alto de Erro.

Having covered a distance of 22 km from Roncesvalles we finally reached Zubiri, our planned stop for the night – only to find all the *hosterias*, *pensiones* and even the €80 per room hotel were full (*'completo'*). This was the long Easter weekend, and we learned that many Spaniards use the opportunity to walk part of the Camino during this period. This explained why there was 'no room at the inns'.

We (Fadi, Greg, Helle, Leonie, Claire, Shivantha and I) finally managed to get accommodation in the municipal hostel located in a former school building. Its three dormitory rooms were full, but they opened up the hall and gave us mattresses (*colchonetas*) to sleep on the floor. Having set these out, we retired to the nearby bar for beers and the €10 pilgrim menu. We were to discover that many of the bars and *albergues* along the Camino offer a cheap pilgrim menu (*menu de peregrinos*) consisting of a soup or salad, a main course of fish or meat, and a simple dessert like yoghurt or ice cream together with wine or water, for about ten to 12 Euros. At the end of a hard day's walk, one is not really in the mood for cooking, so a pilgrim meal is very convenient – and satisfying. We soon realised that the wine offered with these pilgrim meals varied in quality – in some places it was actually very good, at others quite ordinary – so we would often buy a bottle from a supermarket or shop along the way, order the establishment's bottle of water with our meal rather than their wine, and drink our own wine to supplement their water. For four to five Euros I discovered that I could buy a reasonable bottle of Spanish wine in the local supermarkets (*mercados*) – and we were soon learning to enjoy the delightful wines of Navarra and La Rioja with our evening meals.

Friday 22nd April 2011: Zubiri to Pamplona

It was raining this morning when most of those with whom we had spent the night on the floor at the municipal *albergue* in Zubiri left on the next stage of their journey. I had as usual woken up at 5.30 to test my blood sugar, get myself a cup of coffee from the vending machine in the dining room and take my tablets. We shared breakfast with Greg and the others – but after they left we prudently rested until the rain ceased, and left about an hour after they did.

We passed through Larrasoana and then stopped for lunch at a designated picnic area just outside Zubaldica – bread, cheese, sardines, figs and half an excellent bottle of Rioja wine which we had bought at the supermarket at Viskarette and carried with us. Eating the food in our packs was doubly satisfying because it served to lighten the load we had been carrying. What a change this was from my usual lunch break at the clinic in Melbourne, when I would be consuming the contents of a can each of tuna fish and chickpeas while seated at my desk in front of the computer, trying to catch up on correspondence before the afternoon patients started arriving. This had been my routine for so long that I would hardly taste the food as I ingested it – healthy enough food that was easy to carry and did not require preparation, consumed just to replenish the fuel in my tank. Here, in a grassy Spanish *parque* not far away from the river Arga, I was able not only to enjoy a different type of food but also enjoy the leisurely pace at which I was eating and the relaxed conversation we were having while eating.

Shortly after Zubaldica we had to negotiate quite a steep incline, a muddy track that skirted Monte Narval – and the effort was making me begin to feel my years. I slowed my pace of walking – or rather climbing – as, bent forward and using my walking sticks, I took one careful step after the other. I had managed the steep inclines of the Pyrenees a couple of days ago with no major problems – but would this particularly precipitous path be the one that proves too much for my heart and brings on angina?

Shivantha was walking a little ahead of me, but sensing this deceleration of my pace, he dropped back and waited for me to catch up.

"I'll carry your pack for you, *Tha*," he offered.

"Nah, don't worry, I can manage," I replied. How could I expect him to carry my loaded haversack as well as his own pack, which in any case weighed about 17 kg?

It probably pricked my male ego to have to admit that I was old and needed help from my son.

We carried on like this, with Shivantha tactfully slowing his pace to walk behind me as I, step by deliberate step, gradually kept myself moving higher up the path while taking slow deep breaths.

After several minutes, Shivantha came abreast of me and offered once more to carry my pack as well as his so as to allow me an easier ascent. I declined once more – although perhaps my response with a refusal was a little less quick than it was previously.

'OK, *Tha*," he said and moved on ahead of me.

About ten minutes later, he stopped and waited for me, watching me with my head bent and breathing heavily as I used my walking sticks, to slowly help me up the path. In a no-nonsense tone he said firmly, "*Thaththi*, give me your pack" – and I realised that it would be well in my interest to accept his offer.

Shortly thereafter as I, relieved of my burden, ascended the steep incline much more easily, I was most grateful for having my able-bodied son with me, and for having the humility to avail myself of his offer. Interestingly, a short while later we came across (and stopped to talk with) a young Spanish father and his ten-year-old son climbing the same path – with the father stopping to unstrap his son's pack from the little boy's back and strap it onto his own laden back to carry up the incline. When we shared our story with the man, he laughed, "Maybe I can hope when my son Jorge becomes your son's age, he will be able to also carry my pack for me!"

We walked on through little Basque villages with quaint names like Akerreta, Zuriain and Irotz till we reached the *albergue* at Trinidad de Arre, which is situated beside the magnificent medieval stone bridge over the river Urzama. There has been a pilgrim hostel here since the 11th century. Today the monastery hostel is maintained by *Los Hermanos Maristas* (The Marist Brothers) a catholic organisation devoted to the education of children. It was already full, so we got our *Credencials* stamped by the ancient monk seated at the front desk and pushed on through the outskirts of Pamplona, the capital of this region of Navarra. Shortly afterwards we entered the city through the Portal de Francia (again, named for being the entrance through which pilgrims from France entered the city) and made our way to the city centre and the Hotel Vina, where Fadi had booked accommodation for 12 of us at a cheap €14 each.

We realised why the accommodation cost such a little when we opened the door to our room.

In *Lakmahal*, my grandparents' home in Sri Lanka, there were rooms at the back of the house for all the servants. The smallest room furthest from the kitchen was allocated to the gardener, *Thottakkaran* Ayyappan, probably because among the domestic staff he was lowest in the pecking order. He shared this room with his pet cat, his sleeping mat, his gardening tools and his few possessions – and when these were all in the room with him, there was little space for anything or anyone else. I felt that if old Ayyappan had been offered our room at the Hotel Vina, he would have rejected it and left my grandfather's service immediately!

Still, at the end of the day it was good to have some privacy and a place to set down our packs (even if we had to place our packs on top of our boots – and our clothes on top of our packs) and rest. This was in contrast to the previous night in Zubiri where, having reached the town after a long walk, I had to trudge over two kilometres from one '*completo*' establishment to another till we finally managed to get floor space to sleep!

After a shower we ate our evening meal seated on the beds in our room – the rest of the wine together with the leftovers from our lunch plus a tin of Navarese white asparagus, a delicacy of this region. This unusual form of asparagus is produced by piling soil around each plant as it grows so that sunlight does not penetrate into the leaves. The lack of green chlorophyll makes for thick colourless stalks – which are delicious to eat.

Today, despite our route not being over mountains as it had been these past few days, the walk seemed to tire me more. Was it because of the rain that had made our paths muddy? Was it the waning of our initial enthusiasm – or just the fatigue of over-exerted muscles catching up on us? Whatever the explanation, I decided to spend the rest of the evening resting in bed and writing about what we had seen so far in Pamplona - while Shivantha went out with Fadi and the others to have a few drinks and explore the place.

Capital of Spain's autonomous region of Navarra in the Basque country, Pamplona was certainly one of the more interesting cities that we passed through on the Camino.

It is probably best known as the city where the Festival of San Fermin (with its associated *Encierro*, or Running of the Bulls) is held each year in the second week of July. This festival, known as *Sanfermines*, takes place each year from July 6th to 14th – during each morning of which the *Encierro* (made famous by Ernest Hemingway in his 1926 novel *The Sun Also Rises*) is run. Young white-clad men with a surfeit of androgens and adrenaline, wearing red kerchiefs about their necks, race through the streets of the city trying to outrun a dozen fierce bulls - perhaps the most well known event of *Sanfermines*.

But this vibrant city, we discovered, has more to recommend it to visitors than the running of the bulls and the statue of Hemingway outside the *Plaza de Toros* bullring.

Reputed to have been founded in the first century BC by the Roman general Pompey, Pamplona actually grew out of the Basque settlement of Iruña – and over the centuries has witnessed Basque, Roman, Visigoth, Islamic and Catholic rulers, with each of these cultures leaving their influence and imprint on the city and its people.

The city has always been an important place of rest for pilgrims travelling along the French Way (*Via Frances*). In fact, the gateway to the city on the northeast through which we entered Pamplona, just across the Puente de Magdalena bridge over the River Arga, is the one through which pilgrims from France have been entering the city for the past 1,000 years. It is still known as the *Portal de Francia*.

Nowadays, with a population of almost 200,000, Pamplona we found to be a welcoming and modern city, containing many large parks and historical buildings. It is home to one of Spain's finest universities, the Universidad de Navarra, whose picturesque campus covers almost a million square metres.

The Old Quarter San Saturnino is surrounded by ancient walls and watched over by medieval towers. It is a fascinating place of narrow streets, small squares and noble churches – in addition to having some superb places to eat, such as the Bodega a Sarria where we had some delicious *Pinxhos* (Navarrase Tapas) accompanied by some (probably too much) delectable local wine.

Other sites in Pamplona that we found well worth visiting are:

- The Santa María la Real cathedral with its interesting museum and outstanding 13th century cloisters with fine filigree stonework. Inside the cathedral is the 15th century alabaster mausoleum of Navarra's famous King Carlos III and his wife.

- The Plaza del Castillo, the main city square or 'heart of the city', on which many of the narrow lanes of the historical quarter converge. Until 1893, bullfights used to take place here. Surrounded by houses – most of which, with balconies, towers and large picture windows, were built in the 18th century – it is a place to which the local folk go to see and be seen of an evening. The Palace of Navarra, now the seat of government, is situated in this Plaza.

- The Caballo Blanco – certainly one of the most charming corners of Pamplona, beside Plaza de San José and the Cathedral. From here one has magnificent views over the city.

- The Town Hall (*Ayuntamiento*) is situated in the little Plaza Consistorial. Built in the 17th century, its beautiful Baroque façade in dark-coloured stone is crowned by lions bearing coats of arms and a trumpet-blowing angel. The building looks even better at night when it is floodlit.

- The star-shaped citadel, the Ciudadela (which was built during the 16th and 17th centuries to defend the city), is situated within a pleasant park known as the Vuelta del Castillo.

- The many other parks, such La Taconera (which has several monuments to famous personalities, and Louis Paret's neoclassical Fountain of Neptune) and Yamaguchi Park with the planetarium, provide green lungs for the city and pleasant walks for the visitor.

To us from overseas, Pamplona served as a great example of how a medieval city can adapt itself to the needs of the 21st century – without damaging its integral beauty or cultural personality.

Saturday 23rd April 2011: Birthday in Pamplona

We all met for breakfast (coffee and croissants) at a place close to our hotel – and after I was seated, the ladies (Dorval, Julia and Helle) walked in singing *Happy Birthday* and carrying six small cakes with candles on them! What a surprise – I had no idea that Shivantha had informed them it was my 62nd birthday, and I was touched by their gesture.

Father and son decided to spend a rest day in Pamplona, which would allow us to explore the city, so we checked out of our cheap hotel, walked to an internet cafe and booked accommodation at the Hotel Sancho Ramirez through Wotif.com for €69. Along our journey we were to discover that using internet websites such as Wotif.com and Expedia.com was a convenient way to book accommodation – and often got us good discounts off the rack rates.

Although the hotel was about half an hour's walk from the old city, we were very satisfied with the large, clean and comfortable rooms provided. Having showered and washed clothes we took a bus back to the city centre – where, leaving Shivantha to find our *companeros*, I located the El Corte Ingles store and bought myself a Canon Powershot SX210 IS camera for €280 to replace the one I lost in Roncesvalles.

Twenty years ago – even five years ago – I would have baulked at the thought of spending over 300 dollars to buy a camera to replace the camera that I had just a month ago spent 300 dollars to buy. Growing up in Sri Lanka in the Sixties, I had learned to manage with spending as little as possible, the principle we were taught from childhood being that one must always save for a rainy day. On this particular day, however, I made a decision: losing my camera and being deprived of the opportunity of taking photographs of our Camino was definitely a real rainy day, a veritable storm in fact – and after all it WAS my birthday! When later on that day I told Shivantha of the decision I had made, he (who had been most remorseful since we left Roncesvalles, having blamed himself for losing the camera which was at the time in his possession) grinned. "*Tha,*" he observed, "maybe you *are* being changed by the Camino!"

I did a pleasant walk from El Corte Ingles through the Ciudedela back to the old city where we had all arranged to meet at the Plaza Consistorial at 6 pm – and from here we walked to the Bodegon Sarria in Estafeta for some splendid *Pinxhos* and Navarrase wine. It was a great way to celebrate my birthday. Just as in *The Canterbury Tales*, we pilgrims 'broke bread together' and shared our stories:

Greg: from Canada, works for Canada Post and is a keen walker, having hiked through the Rockies and Canada's Arctic regions. He and his wife divorced three years ago. They have no children, but share 'custody' of their two dogs.

Helle: from Funen (*Fyn*) in Denmark, where her father had a glass manufacturing business, which she successfully ran for many years after his death. Now divorced, she has three grown children and works part-time as a psychiatric nurse.

Fadi: the only son of Lebanese parents who lived in Rome and worked there for the Food and Agriculture Organization (FAO). With his parents divorced, Fadi dropped out of university after four years studying Economics and now lives in Paris working with disabled people. He speaks Italian, English, French, Spanish and Arabic – and his dream is to write stories for comic books.

Claire and Leonie: mother and daughter from Brisbane, who had sadly lost their son/brother Matt, aged just 30, to encephalitis last year. What grief and sadness they would have suffered during these past months.

Julia: from Germany, recently qualified doctor who was walking the Camino partly to help her decide whether to break off the relationship she was having with a colleague at her hospital.

After a most enjoyable evening – during which the eight of us consumed six bottles of wine – Shivantha and I took the bus back to our hotel. It was late – but it was too early to go to bed after such an evening – so the two of us had a coffee and chat at the hotel bar before going up to our room. Thanks to the internet, I was able to email and thank all those from home who had sent me good wishes for my birthday.

Chapter 6: The Pole in the Rain

Sunday 24th April 2011: Pamplona to Uterga

We had a leisurely breakfast at the hotel (which provided us with yoghurt and fruit for our lunch) and set off around noon. Soon we reached the campus of the University of Navarra – at the main office of which we were able to get our *Credencials* stamped – and then, having passed through the suburb of Cizur Minor, we came upon a peaceful wooded area where we could hear the calling of birds and buzzing of bees. It was almost as if we were entering a sacred area belonging to Nature. We even came upon a peaceful waterhole reminiscent of the one near Patanangala in Sri Lanka's Yala nature reserve where Shivantha and I had spent many a happy family holiday during his childhood.

It was at Patanangala that one afternoon Shivantha (then five years old) and I had left the rest of the extended family behind at the bungalow where we were all staying and walked along the beach where quite serendipitously we came across one of the most beautiful sights we had seen – the estuary where the river waters met the sea. There were no other humans to be seen – just hordes of colourful butterflies, a group of white storks at the river's edge, a few water buffalo lazily immersing themselves in the warm water, and on the far side a family of elephants contentedly helping themselves to their evening meal of leafy branches broken off the jungle trees.

Holding my hand and with his eyes incredulously wide open, my five-year-old son, who was at the time well versed (thanks to his grandmother) in all the Bible stories, exclaimed, "*Tha*, is this The Promised Land?"

This 'Promised Land' in Yala became part of our family folklore – one of those treasured memories that father and son share and years later still reminisce about. I used to say that when I finally pass away, I would like him to take my ashes and return them to the earth at this place in Yala.

And now on the Camino, so many thousand miles away from Yala and Sri Lanka, father and son stopped for a while to savour the scenery – and reminisce about a faraway time and a place that we called The Promised Land.

From here our route climbed upwards to the summit of the Hill of Forgiveness *(Alto de Perdon)* with its metal sculpture of windswept pilgrims and a row of wind turbines that emphasise the importance Spain places on eco-power. While we were making our way down from the summit it started to rain – a drizzle of raindrops at first which soon turned into pelting cold rain. We put on our raincoats and, with raindrops smudging our spectacles (why has no one yet invented windscreen wipers for spectacles?), trudged downward along the muddy path.

It was here that we came across a man fallen by the side of the path. When we saw this human form covered in a blue raincoat lying in a muddy puddle, with the rain falling on him and the muddy water trickling downhill and soaking him, my first thought was, "Is this creature alive?" We stopped, and when we were able to make out the rise and fall of the man's breathing, we roused him and asked if he needed help. Although we repeatedly offered to help him get up – me asking in English and Spanish and Shivantha in French and Italian - he said he was OK and declined our offer of assistance. I decided to leave him and walk on – there is little we can do to help a person who rejects our offer of help – but my son was not happy, and even after we left the fallen pilgrim Shivantha kept turning around to look at the man, still lying inebriated in the mud with the rain falling around him and the muddy water trickling past him.

As we kept walking and Shivantha kept turning round to look, we saw the three Austrian pilgrims who had been some distance behind us stopping to talk to the man. When Shivantha saw the man shakily getting to his feet, he turned around, left me and walked back to the spot.

The next thing I saw was Shivantha marching back towards me, carrying his own pack on his back – and the man's pack (soaked with water and cowdung) strapped to the front of my son's chest! Supported by the old Austrian, the man himself was staggering along. I could see him shivering and his teeth chattering. Like this the two of us and the three old Austrians (a man and two ladies) walked on with him till we came to the *albergue* at Camino del Perdon in Uterga, where we checked in and handed the man we had found in the rain to the care of the *hospitaleros* in the *albergue*. As we picked up our packs to go to our rooms, he turned to Shivantha, raised his hand and said slowly, "Thank you much"- which probably represented almost all the words of English he knew. The incident reminded me of the Biblical parable of the Good Samaritan – the only difference being that my son did not offer to pay for the man's board and lodging at the inn.

The man, we discovered, was named Jasek, a pilgrim from Poland who for some reason which we never discovered had gone out from the *albergue* that afternoon and had been seen seated by the path with a cask of white wine which he had apparently consumed completely.

Thanks to Fadi, our group – now increased to 12 - had a five-roomed house to ourselves at the cost of €50 for each very comfortable room. The others gave us the biggest room which had two beds and an attached bathroom with Jacuzzi. This was exactly what Shivantha needed to clean himself of the mud and dirt he had acquired carrying the drunken man's pack!

We finished the day with a hearty pilgrim dinner at the Camino del Perdon *albergue* – steaming lentil soup, fried trout, apple tart with ice cream and some very acceptable red wine. While seated at dinner we saw our Polish friend, now cleaned up and looking warm, seated at a table by himself having dinner (without wine). He looked much healthier than he did when we first saw him – and managed to give us a smile and a wave.

My son had taught me Camino Lesson Number Four: ***Along the Camino – as along the journey of Life – be ever prepared to help a stranger in distress. Even those who may reject your initial offer of assistance can be helped.***

Monday 25th April 2011: Uterga to Mañeru

We left Uterga around 9.30 am, having decided to walk to Eunate in order to visit the famous Church of Santa Maria there. This involved a detour from the main Camino path, but the extra effort proved well worthwhile.

The 12th century Romanesque church in Eunate stands alone in the open countryside, the only building nearby being a small private house where the church guardians live. With its octagonal structure, three-sided apse, three groups of windows and unembellished interior – typical Templar architectural features – this beautifully simple church has long been associated with the Knights Templar, the '*Poor Fellow-Soldiers of Christ and of the Temple of Solomon*' who between the 12th and 14th centuries are known to have provided protection for pilgrims along the way to Santiago de Compostela. The church itself is built of smooth ashlars (dressed stone blocks) and is surrounded by a peaceful cloister – the whole enclosed by a freestanding circular outer porch made up of delicate twin pillars.

We stopped for a while to admire the church, and witnessed a group of French pilgrims reverently entering the church, lighting candles, praying – and then spending a while singing songs of devotion within the little church.

The Way took us from Eunate on to Puente La Reina, a town of about 2,500 inhabitants which is where the two tributaries of the Camino – the French Way (along which we had come from St Jean Pied de Port) and the Aragonese way (which passes from France into Spain through the more southern Somport Pass over the Pyrenees) – join up. Puente La Reina means 'Bridge of the Queen', the town being named after the magnificent Romanesque stone bridge over the river Arga that was built in the 11th century on the instructions of Dona Mayor, wife of the great Navarrese King Sancho III.

We stopped for a bite – tortilla and *pinxhos* with Damm Limon beer shandy at the pleasant Restaurant Jakue – before continuing on our way, walking with a young Spanish pilgrim, a teacher who grew up in Sansol. We had an interesting discussion with him, the topics ranging from growing up in Sansol to growing up in Sri Lanka, from Tamil Tigers to the Basque ETA group.

He, a Spaniard and a Basque named Xavier, had spent his childhood in a country which was dominated by the majority Castilian Spaniards – under whose subjugation lived Catalans, Galicians and Basques, minority groups that spoke different languages and considered themselves culturally different from the Castilians. Under the 26 year dictatorship of General Francisco Franco, Castilians dominated the nation and the minorities felt themselves suppressed, forced to assimilate and give up their language in deference to Castilian Spanish. Our young friend, a Navarrese Basque, belonged to the minority group who believed they had been most discriminated against by the majority Castilians and from whose number had arisen ETA, or *Euskadi ta Askatasuna*, the separatist organisation waging an armed struggle against Spain's central government.

Shivantha and I, on the other hand, had grown up in Sri Lanka as Sinhalese – belonging to the majority group in a country comprising Sinhalese, Tamils, Moors, Malays and Burghers. The largest of the minority groups in our country are the Tamils, ethnically and linguistically different from the Sinhalese. Moreover, unlike the different cultural groups of Spain who are all Roman Catholics, the different ethnic groups in Sri Lanka belong to different religious groups – the Sinhalese being mainly Buddhist, the Tamils predominantly Hindu, the Moors and Malays Moslem, and the Burghers (those of mixed European and Sri Lankan ancestry) Christian – of both Catholic and Protestant denominations.

In any situation where a minority group perceives that it is being discriminated against by the majority, some people in that group will come to believe, and then start trying to convince others, that their only hope is armed conflict – and from just such a situation in Sri Lanka was born a separatist group calling itself the Liberation Tigers of Tamil Eelam, better known as the LTTE or Tamil Tigers.

This group brought a whole new dimension to the business of guerrilla warfare. Long before US President George W. Bush realised what terrorism was and promulgated a much publicised 'War on Terror' – in fact, long before Bush could spell the word 'terrorist' – the Tamil Tigers, fighting to establish a separate state in Sri Lanka, had elevated terrorism to a fine art. Female suicide bombers, the suicide bra, child soldiers, targeted assassination of political and military leaders including those of their own ethnic group who the Tigers believed were not wholeheartedly with them – all these were part of the armamentarium of the LTTE. Sri Lanka's military triumph against this terrorist group in 2009 has been an inspiration for many other countries beset by highly motivated, heavily armed and externally funded separatist groups.

Chatting with our new friend from Sansol as we walked gave all of us a fresh perspective on this subject of how the nations of the 21st century will have to exist with the reality of multiculturalism. Will the Basques occupying northeast Spain continue to agitate for a 'homeland' – and will they try to join up with the Basque people in Southwest France? Did the military victory of 2009 spell the end of the Tamil Tigers' quest for a separate state in Sri Lanka – or will it resurface if the government does not address the factors that spawned the separatist group in the first place? Is it better for separate ethnic groups to compromise and live together in a federal state or go it alone as an ethnically homogenous nation – as the Pakistanis did with the break-up of British India, as the various nations of the former Yugoslavia did following the disintegration of that country, and as the Kurds and the Chechens and so many other groups who consider themselves different from their countrymen seem to be trying to do?

We hardly noticed the kilometres being walked as we shared our views – and at about three in the afternoon we reached Maneru, a sleepy little village which marked a hundred kilometres since we had commenced our journey in St Jean Pied de Port.

Here we found a relatively new and small *albergue* – six bunk beds with showers and a patio enclosed by an ancient high wall. The cost was only €10 each for bed, breakfast and the added benefit of free use of the internet. The *albergue* was managed by a bearded *hospitalero* called Naxho, a pleasant and obliging man who reminded me of a plump Mexican bandit. After our discussion that morning, I could not suppress the sneaking suspicion that he might even have been a Basque terrorist/ freedom fighter in the days when he was younger and slimmer.

Having cleaned off the dirt of our journey we decided to avail ourselves of the dinner Naxho was offering for an extra €10. He cooked us a meal – eggs, chorizo, bacon and ham for me, and a bowl of tripe for Shivantha. With each savoured mouthful I could almost visualise the cholesterol congealing inside my arteries – but I justified the unhealthy diet by convincing myself that our five-hour walk that day would have burned up more than enough of my body's sugar and cholesterol. After the meal we opened the bottle of red wine that I had carried from Uterga and sat outside in the walled courtyard into which the evening sunlight gently streamed down. We leisurely finished the bottle between us, father and son, while (like the walrus and the carpenter in Lewis Carroll's famous poem) we talked of many things.

It had been a long time since Shivantha and I had been able to sit down and have a chat. With him having spent the past three years in New York, working for a degree from the American Academy of Dramatic Arts, and me having been in Melbourne, working in the clinic, teaching at university and doing time with the Australian Army Reserve, we had not really had the opportunity of having time to ourselves to talk. Sure, telephones are convenient and, with phone cards and communication plans, relatively cheap – while Skype with its ability to transmit real-time images has revolutionised the whole business of keeping in touch; but none of these can substitute for chatting face-to-face without a time limit. And when the conversation is punctuated and memories are facilitated by the glasses of Rioja reds in our hands – how much better can it get?

I recall an evening several years ago when I was seated with my wife, my parents and a 16-year-old Shivantha on the balcony of my grandparents' home on a particularly hot April evening in Colombo. There had been a week-long strike by the power company during that time, and in a home that had got used to electric lights, fans, air conditioners, refrigerators and televisions, this was most inconvenient. But it forced us to occupy our evenings seated out on the relatively cool balcony, with candles and kerosene lanterns for light, spending the time devoid of televisions, radios and even artificial light for reading by engaging in conversation. “Come,” my father used to say on those evenings, motioning to one of us to carry his armchair out into the balcony, “let’s have a chat.” And one particular observation of his that day I have remembered all these years. “This is just like the days when we were small,” he said, “as evening fell, my father would be seated in his reclining chair with his big mug of tea, we children would sit on mats on the ground around him, old Carolis the servant would bring out a couple of old ashtrays bearing lighted candles that he would set on the balustrade – and we would spend the hour or two before mother called us for dinner just chatting and sharing the activities of the day.”

I believe that with modern methods of communication we are losing the art of conversation. It is bad enough that families nowadays are no longer as extended as they were a hundred years ago, with children losing the privilege of spending childhood in the presence of grandparents. Even in ‘normal’ families, we spend our leisure time watching television where we are fed information and entertainment by those who control and manipulate the media. We communicate through mobile phones and computers – and communication is by texting rather than conversing.

Sitting out here in the courtyard of Naxho’s *albergue* at Maneru (clean, comfortable and probably the simplest accommodation we had stayed in so far), father and son were able to converse, communicate – and connect.

Tuesday 26th April 2011: Maneru to Estella

Leaving Naxho’s *albergue* we walked out through the sleepy streets of Maneru, passing on the outskirts of town a cemetery with an unusual wrought-iron cross. We then made our way through the narrow winding streets of the medieval hilltop village of Ciraqui (sometimes referred to as the Vipers' Nest!), then a second quaint village Lorca, and finally the small town of Villatuerta before we reached the town of Estella. Here we found the Hotel Cristina, where with my increasing fluency in Spanish (forced on me by necessity) I had managed to book accommodation for the two of us. The hotel had obviously seen better days, but for €45 we had a room with two beds to ourselves. We cleaned ourselves and walked to the nearby *lavanderia* (laundry) where we gave a big bundle of dirty clothes to be washed – and then to the Farmacia Eccheverria where the pharmacist, Mrs Rosa Maria Eccheverria, was most helpful regarding Shivantha's troublesome left knee. He got himself some Voltaren gel and a knee guard – and we were walking back towards our hotel when we noticed a small kebab shop. It was run by a Pakistani man, so we bought some kebab pitas (with extra chili) and drinks and then went for a look around the town.

We availed ourselves of the opportunity to visit the old palace of the Kings of Navarra in Estella. The Romanesque building is now an art museum, and had an exhibition of paintings by Guztavo de Maeztu, the famous artist who spent much of his life in Estella and gifted his paintings to the city shortly before he died there. Facing the royal palace is the *Iglesia San Pedro de la Rua*, rising high on a cliff. Unfortunately the church, which is reputed to have a beautiful cloister, was closed for repairs.

Estella became affluent thanks to the many pilgrims who passed this way along the Camino. During the 11th century the city was granted special privileges by the king, and this attracted settlers from other parts of Europe whose skills as artists and craftsmen helped build the many churches, bridges and monuments that are evident today. The picturesque Rio Aga flows through the city, and in medieval times the area south of the river had separate boroughs for the various nationalities that settled here – French, Jewish and so on.

In the afternoon Shivantha, Greg and I sat in the Plaza Fueros, the bustling main square with its many cafes, just having a beer and watching the locals enjoying the spring afternoon. Fadi and Claire joined us later for an hour or so. Later still, while Shivantha went off with the young ones, Greg and I strolled through the cobbled streets until we found a restaurant to have a nice quiet meal – *bacalao* (cod) for me and calamari in black sauce for him.

Wednesday 27th April 2011: Estella to Los Arcos

I was at the bar in the Plaza Fueros by 7.30 am to have the *Desayuno Especiale* (special breakfast) of orange juice, chocolate croissant and coffee. This is the standard morning fare in Spain – quite different to the coffee, Weetbix, yoghurt and fruit with which we are used to starting off the day in Melbourne.

I visited the post office as it opened its doors at 8.30 to post back home a large envelope of my things which over the past week I had decided were surplus to my requirements – notepapers, scarf, beanie, marker pens, extra bathers, camera wires and the electronic translator that my friend Hermann had kindly lent me for the trip. The post office staff appeared quite accustomed to this sort of request – we met a couple more pilgrims at the same post office posting stuff home. Estella seems to be the place, about 120 km and one week into the journey, where folk realise that every gram they have with them has to be carried on their back for another 700 km and five weeks all the way to Santiago. A good time and place to make the decision – what is essential for my journey, what can I discard? It cost me €20 – but I looked on it as 20 Euros spent for prophylactic medicine to prevent myself developing back problems.

Greg, Shivantha and I left the Hotel around 9.30 and made our way through the medieval city gate of Estella, the *Puerta de Castilla* to reach the Bodega de Irache winery because we had heard about their famous wine fountain. This is a fountain maintained by the winery; the fountain has two taps from which pilgrims can refresh themselves – one yielding water and the other wine. Above the fountain is a plaque which says '*Peregrino, si quieres llegar a Santiago con fuerza y vitalidad de este gran vino echa un trago y brinda por la felicidad*' ('Pilgrim, if you wish to arrive at Santiago full of strength and vitality, have a drink of this great wine and raise a toast to happiness').

Needless to say we drank our fill and filled a bottle each for the road.

From here it was about 3 km to the little village of Azqueta which we reached around noon. Just before entering Azqueta we passed the 13th century Fountain of the Moors (*Fuente de Los Moros*). Built into the hill, this is a square structure with a distinctive Mozarabic double-arched entrance. Inside there are steps leading down to a rectangular pool that is fed by spring water dripping in from one corner and gradually overflowing into a square well in the centre of the pool.

The Mozarabs were Christians (converts from Islam and Judaism or migrants from northern Spain who moved south) who lived in the relatively tolerant Moslem kingdoms of Southern Spain, *al-Andalus,* during Spain's seven centuries of Islamic rule. Although allowed to practise their own religion, they embraced the language and culture of the Islamic society in which they lived – and their artistic and architectural influence can still be seen in various medieval buildings in many parts of Spain.

Azqueta was resting during its afternoon siesta by the time we reached it. The government office was deserted – closed for lunch – so we decided to sprawl ourselves on the steps leading up to its main entrance and have our meal of brown bread, cheese, chorizo, yoghurt and the wine from the Bodega de Irache that we had in our bottles. After this we too needed a siesta for about half an hour before we were able to start walking again.

Our next stop was the small village of Villamayor de Monjardin, where I was keen to visit the 12th century St Andres church whose high tower can be seen for miles around. Its doors have well preserved medieval iron work – but the highlight in this church is the Processional Cross of Monjardin. This wooden cross, about 75 cm tall, is laminated in silver and has an image of Christ whose body is perfectly sculpted anatomically with the pathos of the Crucifixion expressively carved into the face.

Why, I thought to myself as I gazed at this, does Spanish Christianity depict the suffering of Christ and the saints in so many of its works of art? Places of worship belonging to other religions are so different – Buddhist temples from Japan to Sri Lanka have serene statues of the Buddha in poses of meditation, contemplation, teaching or even laughter, the colourful paintings and lifelike sculptures inside Hindu temples celebrate the activities of normal human life (even to the extent of depicting the very act of joyous sexual union in temples like those in Khajuraho, India) while Jewish synagogues and Islamic mosques refrain from showing any human images inside them. Why then do the gloomy churches of Spain emphasise so much this aspect of suffering? There is always the image of Christ nailed to a horrible Roman instrument of torture that was designed to inflict a slow and painful death – as well as paintings of so many saints in various states of suffering: being stoned to death, pierced by arrows, stretched out on the wheel, having their breasts cut off or being flayed alive. What purpose do all these gruesome images of nasty things being done to good people have in emphasising Christ's basic message of loving your neighbour and doing good to others? Were they intended to put fear into the people so they would do as they were told by those who wielded the power of church and state?

Leaving the sobering church in Villamayor we walked along remote farm tracks that passed through wheat fields, vineyards and olive groves for about ten kilometres until we finally reached the town of Los Arcos at about five in the evening. We had walked for almost six hours and were now ready for our rest – and made our way to the Albergue Isaac Santiago, maintained by a Flemish fraternity.

After dinner we wandered around the narrow streets, soaking in the peace and tranquillity of this ancient town which has been a classic resting place for pilgrims over the years. Nearing a church with a splendid Romanesque bell tower and an impressive Gothic cloister – the 12th century Church of St Mary of the Arches (*Iglesia de Santa Maria de los Arcos)* – we could hear melodious chanting emanating from within. On entering, we discovered the music was from a group of French pilgrims – the same ones we had met previously at the church in Eunate – and spent the better part of an hour listening to them, our fatigue temporarily forgotten, before wending our weary way to the Albergue.

Thursday 28th April 2011: Los Arcos to Viana

At 6 am we were woken by the sound of a church bell and lights coming on in the dormitory. The *albergue hospitaleros* obviously felt that they needed to get us up and out in time to clean up for the next day's arrivals.

We left at 7.45 without a formal breakfast – although I polished off a whole tin of Navarrase asparagus that I had with me to avoid walking on an empty stomach – and walked the 7 km to Sansol where we had coffee, tortillas and bananas. We walked up to the area behind the church (as Xavier our Sansolian friend had advised us to do) and were treated to a breathtaking view of the surrounding area.

The next stop was Torres del Rio. Here we stopped at the Church of the Holy Sepulchre – like the church at Eunate, it has the distinctive octagonal shape and simple interior associated with the Knights Templar – to discover the same French group we had met twice previously singing their songs of praise inside the church. Unlike many of those we have met walking The Way so far, these were obviously good Catholic pilgrims, singing their way to Santiago!

Soon after we left Torres del Rio, we met an Australian couple walking back from Santiago. They were from Byron Bay and, having met their daughter in Santiago, were walking the Camino in the reverse direction. It was good to hear an Aussie accent again – and to hear their frank advice ("That was a shithouse plyce, myte!") about some of the accommodation *en route*.

We walked on, chatting with Greg who knows so much about various different topics – movies, cycling, physical fitness – until we reached the town of Viana around two in the afternoon. The *albergue* into which we checked today, Albergue Andres Munoz, was originally a monastery that was acquired and converted into a pilgrim hostel. The novelty here was that it had three-tiered bunks. After the usual shower and clothes-washing routine we went on to the hostel terrace, which provided a fine view of the route we would follow tomorrow to Logrono, and then walked to a bar where we had a late lunch of bocadillos and beers, served by a Romanian girl who was able to converse in six languages.

Following a short nap we decided to have a good dinner because it would be our last night with Greg, who would leave us in Logrono the following day to head for Barcelona and then home to Canada. The three of us walked to the Palacio de Pujadas (which certainly looked as if it had once been somebody's palace, now tastefully restored) and had a memorable farewell meal in their restaurant *Portillo*.

Viana is an interesting town, its historical centre little changed from when pilgrims of the medieval age were walking through on their way to Santiago. The town has an association with Cesare

Borgia, the illegitimate son of Rodrigo Borgia of the famous (or infamous) Borgia family of Aragon. After Rodrigo was elected Pope in 1492 – he ruled with the name Pope Alexander VI and is remembered as one of the most corrupt holders of that office – Cesare was appointed commander of the Papal armies. On Pope Alexander's death in 1503, his successor Pope Pius III prudently banished Cesare to Spain, where he died defending Viana during the siege of 1507. His tombstone can be seen in front of Viana's *Iglesia de Santa Maria* (Church of Saint Mary).

The famous Basque writer Navarro Villoslada was born in Viana; we saw the house in which he lived, which is now the local library.

Chapter 7: The Kindness of Strangers

Friday 29th April 2011: Viana to Navarette

On Friday morning we left Viana after the usual breakfast of coffee and croissants and passed out of the town through the medieval stone arch Portal San Felices. Accompanied by Greg, we crossed two small rivers, the Valdearas and the Labraza, and hiked on past the Cantano de las Canas nature reserve towards Logrono. We were now leaving the region of Navarra and crossing into the small but famous wine-producing region of La Rioja.

At the site of the Puente de Piedra stone bridge that goes over the river Ebro into the city of Logrono we stopped. Seated on the grassy bank of the river we had a picnic lunch of cheese, chorizo, olives, olive bread and (although we had crossed by now into La Rioja) a bottle of Navarra wine. We bade an emotional farewell to Greg – he was going to take the 5 pm train that day from Logrono to Barcelona and then fly on home to Canada the following day. He had been with us from the start of our journey ten days previously, and had been a good companion to us in this journey.

Will we ever see him again? I don't know – but somehow I feel we shall. I certainly know that we are going to miss his company.

Crossing the Puente de Piedra into Logrono, the capital of the autonomous region of La Rioja, we walked on through this lively university town and then past the picturesque reservoir of Plantano de la Grajera to reach Navarette around 4.30 pm. We had walked about 22 km since leaving Viana, a total of five-and-a-half hours.

We checked into the municipal hostel, and then had a beer out in the square with Sjoerd and Ann from South Africa. For a change we decided today to cook dinner in the hostel kitchen and so joined forces with Ian and June from Devon. Most of the cooking was done by June - although Ian and I *did* help with the cutting up and Shivantha did the washing up. We had a pleasant meal (accompanied by the very ordinary bottles of wine that Ian and I had selected from the *supermercado*) and an enjoyable chat at the table about various topics ranging from art and teaching to children and life in general.

The autonomous region of La Rioja is sandwiched between the mountainous Basque region of Navarra to the northeast and the flat *meseta* of the Leon and Castille region to the west. It was near Logrono that the famous battle of Clavijo was fought in 844 AD – the legendary battle between the Moors (who in the year 711 had invaded Spain from North Africa and were extending their kingdoms northwards) and the Catholic Spaniards (who were trying to regain control of their country). Legend has it that at Clavijo, the Spaniards led by King Ramiro I of Castile were battling the Moslem forces led by the Emir of Cordoba. The battle was going against the Spaniards when St James (Santiago) himself appeared from the sky mounted on a white charger. Ferociously attacking the Moorish army, he is held to have slaughtered hundreds of enemy soldiers and helped turn the tide of battle against the Moors.

This was a time in history when the fortunes of the Christian kingdoms in Spain were at a low ebb – in fact they were facing the Moslem invaders with their backs to the wall. They needed an inspirational champion – and in the legend of *Santiago Matamoros* (St James the Moorslayer) they were presented with a powerful champion and patron saint.

One result of the Battle of Clavijo was that Santiago started gaining a reputation as *El Matamoros* – and it is in this guise (one might even call it an avatar, as in the case of the Hindu gods) that he is depicted in many works of art. Even in the Plaza de Obradoiro, the huge plaza of Santiago de Compostela, the façade of the cathedral has a large statue of St James in his usual avatar of a pilgrim, clad in his wide-brimmed hat with the traditional scallop shell and carrying his staff and gourd of water – while on the opposite side of the plaza, the front of the neoclassical Pazo de Raxoi, which is now the town hall, is surmounted by a huge statue of Santiago the Moorslayer, brandishing his sword while a group of terrified Moslems is being trampled beneath the hooves of his charger.

To me, the depictions of St James as both *Santiago Matamoros*, the Moorslayer, and as *Santiago Peregrino*, the Pilgrim, make a mockery of intelligent thought. How could this man James, the son of Zebedee and Jesus' mother's sister Salome, a man who in life had been a chosen disciple of Jesus Christ and a humble fisherman of Nazareth during the first century AD, a man who preached the 'Love thy neighbour as thyself' and 'Turn the other cheek' messages of Christ, suddenly appear out of the sky in the ninth century AD to champion the case of a warring Spanish king and ruthlessly slaughter Moslems? Even more ridiculous is the depiction of St James as a pilgrim on his way to Santiago de Compostela, dressed in pilgrim garb and scallop shell-emblazoned hat, wending his way along the Camino to pay his respects to his own bones that are enshrined in the relic chamber of the cathedral.

It certainly beggars belief. This is why, as I said earlier, I have the greatest respect for the founders of religion like Jesus Christ, Prophet Mohamed and the Buddha, and nothing but cynicism and mistrust for those purveyors of institutionalised religion who feed the gullible masses with priest-crafted myths of religion – about Moorslayers sent by God and saints who make pilgrimages to their own graves.

Saturday 30th April 2011: Navarette to Ventosa

We had our usual Spanish breakfast at the local bar in Navarette and left at 8.45. Shivantha's foot however was giving him a lot of pain, and by the time we were approaching the small village of Ventosa he was limping badly. Although it was just 11.30 and we had only walked some 8 km today, we decided that we would stop here for the night to give him a chance to rest. Unfortunately, the Albergue San Saturnino – from the outside it looked a very peaceful and well maintained small pilgrim hostel – did not open until 2 pm, so we had no alternative but to sit outside on their doorstep to patiently wait.

While we were waiting, I decided to look for a shop to buy some food – at least some milk and bread and ham, as we were quite hungry having had only coffee and *napolitanas* for breakfast. I walked along the narrow streets up to and beyond the village square for about half an hour, but there were very few people about and everything appeared closed. The village square was deserted, the one shop I could find firmly closed and shuttered.

As I was returning empty-handed back to the *albergue* I came across an old lady standing outside her house. I asked her in my limited Spanish whether there was a shop in the village where I could buy some food. She listened patiently – and then not only walked with me to the house of the local chorizo-seller located off a tiny side street where I purchased some delicious locally made chorizo, but (because there were apparently no shops in Ventosa that sell processed milk) she walked with me to the coffee bar further on and bought a litre of milk which she then gave to me, refusing any money. I later discovered from Shivantha that while I was gone she had seen him seated at the *albergue* entrance and bought a baguette of bread from the passing bread vendor which she had given to him, again refusing any payment.

We were touched by her generosity – typical of the village folk who since ancient times have been helping pilgrims along the Camino, displaying what it is to be helpful to their fellow human beings.

The chorizo, bread and milk relieved our hunger until the *albergue hospitalera* opened the place around two. We were the first in and settled into the place. After a shower I gave Shivantha a foot massage with Tiger Balm and placed a heat pack on his painful foot. Leaving him to rest in bed with his injured foot elevated on his pack, I walked to the bar for a bite. Here I sat with three pilgrims from Madrid - Julio, Carlos and Kaki. Carlos had been walking from Catalonia; he had already done 400 km and was continuing from here to Santiago de Compostela along the Via Primitiva, the route that goes northwards and then parallel to the coast through Bilbao, Santander and Oviedo. His eyesight, he told me, was failing – possibly due to hypertensive retinopathy or glaucoma – and he was walking now because "in five years I may not see well enough to walk." Julio was a telecommunications engineer who was made redundant in his job last year, and was using this opportunity to "do what I have always wanted to do but did not have the time for."

Talking with them in that peculiar combination of English, Spanish and hand gestures that is typical of our communications with fellow pilgrims along the Camino, I realised that being diagnosed with a terminal or debilitating illness, losing one's job, experiencing a crisis in one's life – all these can be devastating; but once one comes to terms with the initial shock, they can be taken as opportunities that open up gateways to new and fruitful paths.

Here was Camino Lesson Number Five: ***When disaster strikes, instead of looking at what you can no longer do, look instead at what you now have the opportunity to try. Change***

your perspective -- and the limitations that have been imposed on you become an incentive to seize new opportunities.

Our journey along this road was giving me the opportunity to learn so much. This knowledge comes not as a dramatic revelation such as St Paul had on the road to Damascus nor even in the form of sudden enlightenment as the Buddha achieved under the *pipul* (*bo*) tree in Bodhgaya. I daresay that wisdom will not strike me as I walk through the cathedral doors in Santiago at the end of this journey – or even if I butt my head against the statue of Maestro Mateo at the cathedral entrance in the pilgrim's age-old ritual of *Santo d'os Croques* (touching one's forehead to that of the saint) to receive some of his genius. I am gradually realising that after this journey I will be wiser and more attuned to living well as a result of meeting – and listening – to so many others along the Camino. I recall a line in Tennyson's poem *Ulysses*:

'I am a part of all that I have met...'

For me, who has spent most of his life trying to instruct others – telling patients what to do, giving soldiers orders and lecturing to students (and using the same approach that I use for patients, soldiers and students in dealing with my children) – this journey is teaching me for a change to Listen.

And I am sure the change is doing me good.

Sunday 1st May 2011: Ventosa to Najera

Morning came and Shivantha's foot was not back to normal, so we decided to take a taxi from Ventosa to our next destination, Najera.

Early that morning I decided that I should go and find the kind lady who had helped us – the strange dark pilgrims from

Plate 9

9A: Mi Padre – poster in Astorga

9B: Sculpture of Father and Son in Leon

Plate 10

10 A: Sculpture of Father and Son in Burgos

10 B: By the river Burbia at Villafranca del Bierzo

Plate 11

11A: Father and Son at the end of a day's walking

11B: Final waymarker (Finisterre)

Plate 12

12A: Botofumeiro at Santiago Cathedral

12B: Journey's end – in front of the cathedral at Santiago de Compostela

Sri Lanka – the previous day. Ventosa being a small place, it was not difficult for the *hospitalera* to tell me, from my description of the lady, where she lived. I walked to her place and rang the bell – and when she came downstairs, I gave her a picture postcard on which I had written in Spanish: '*Thank you for your kindness to us. From the two pilgrims, the father and son, from Sri Lanka*'. It was the least I could do to express our gratitude and acknowledge the kindness she had shown to us, two complete strangers, when we were in need – and I could see that she was touched by the gesture and appreciated my coming back to say "Thank You".

While we waited for the car (probably the only hiring car in Ventosa!) to arrive, we had a chat with Juta, the *hospitalera* at the Albergue San Saturnino. She gave us some useful advice: "Do not worry about deadlines, because you will finish the Camino in the time you have set yourselves. You do not have to push yourselves – the journey will take care of you."

Her words echoed the lesson that we were learning along the Camino. While reaching your destination is important, the destination should not be the sole purpose of your journey. What is important is to live in the present and to enjoy the journey.

The ride by car, which cost us €22, was a little over 9 km and took us less than half an hour. Our destination was the Hotel San Fernando in Najera, just next to the bus station; while we were in Ventosa I had used Shivantha's laptop to make a reservation there. We sat in the hotel foyer and read until the room was made ready for us, then carried our packs up to our comfortable room and adjourned to the hotel bar to have breakfast. After this I left Shivantha to rest and went for a walk over the bridge to explore the old town, the ancient capital of the Kingdom of Navarra in the 11th and 12th centuries. The name Najera is derived from the Arabic *Naxara* (place among the rocks) and comes from the time a thousand years ago when all this area was under Moslem rule.

From the bridge over the river Najerilla the old town could be seen against its dramatic background of a tall and craggy wall of red rock.

Today, May 1st, happened to be the anniversary of the day in 1217 when King Ferdinand III (Fernando the Saint, or *Fernando el Santo*) was proclaimed King of Castile. The coronation had taken place in Najera, and each year the event is commemorated with a grand procession. I was lucky to have the opportunity of witnessing this festive musical parade of folk dressed in colourful medieval costumes winding its way through the city. There were kings and queens, priests and pilgrims, musicians playing their instruments and Arabic dancers waving their scimitars – all very lively with everyone, costumed participants as well as spectators, thoroughly enjoying themselves.

Having watched the procession I visited the *Monasterio Santa Maria del Real*, with its beautiful Cloister of the Knights and the Royal Pantheon housing the tombs of the kings and queens of Navarra. Of particular beauty here is the tomb of Queen Blanca of Castille and Navarra, who died in childbirth. The carvings at the base of her sarcophagus show the Queen on her deathbed and the grieving King being supported by his knights.

That evening we decided to have a good meal – so meeting up with Fadi, Leonie, Claire and Julia, we went to the Meson de Manu for a delicious (though expensive) meal.

Yesterday and today were days of 'taking it easy' – forced on us, perhaps, by Shivantha's injured foot – but something I am glad we did on this journey. Walking continuously, seven days a week and hell-bent on getting to one's destination in the shortest possible time, should not be the aim of the Camino.

Camino Lesson Number Six: ***Take your time, make sure you do not forget to rest and relax and enjoy your surroundings –***

and the journey will take care of itself. The pleasure of walking to Santiago is as much in the journey as in the destination.

Monday 2nd May 2011: Najera to Santo Domingo de Calzada

I went for an early morning stroll through the streets of Najera, even dropping into the *Centro de Salud* (Health Centre) to have a look around before the patients arrived. I then had breakfast in the hotel by myself and later sat with Shivantha (who woke up later) to keep him company while he had his breakfast. We then walked to the post office where he mailed back home (as I had done a few days previously in Estella) a package containing the excess baggage that he had brought from New York. It weighed about 2 kg and cost him €38 – but I advised him to look on it as paying €38 for preventive health care – a sum that would be less than what it would cost him to consult a doctor and buy medicines if his foot continued to give him trouble.

How the monetary value one places on things changes as one proceeds along the Camino...

We took our time packing and checked out of the hotel in time to walk to the bus stand just in front of our hotel and take the 11.50 bus to San Domingo de Calzada. The 21 km trip took us just half an hour and cost only €1.43. We checked into the Abadia Cisterciense, a peaceful hostel run by Cistercian nuns, and managed to reserve beds there for Fadi, Leonie, Claire and Julia who were walking from Najera and arrived around 3.45 pm.

This little town with its winding streets is named after a man who became famous as Saint Dominic of the Causeway (*Santo Domingo de Calzada*). In the 11th century he was responsible for building in this place not only the original pilgrim hostel (now the luxurious Parador) and the church which is now the local cathedral, but also many of the surrounding roads and bridges along which pilgrims travel to Santiago de Compostela. Legend has it that he was born to a humble peasant family in these parts, and when he applied to become a monk of the Benedectine order at the monastery of San Millan he was rejected because he was illiterate.

The town named after him is also famous for another legend – that of the chickens who came back to life.

This legend goes back to the time when a pilgrim couple and their son from Germany who were on their way to Santiago de Compostela stopped at the local inn for the night. The innkeeper's daughter cast her eye on the handsome young man – but he, being the devout pilgrim that he was, resisted her advances. Scorned by his rejection (as in the famous and often misquoted lines from William Congreve's play 'Heaven has no rage like love to hatred turned / Nor hell a fury like a woman scorned') the girl that night hid a silver goblet in his pack while he was asleep. When he left the next morning she reported him as having stolen it. The lad was caught, his pack searched – and when the missing goblet was found inside his pack he, although he protested his innocence, was condemned to death by hanging.

His parents continued on their pilgrimage, unaware of their son's fate – but travelling back home through the town on their return from Santiago de Compostela, they found him hanging from the gallows. Miraculously, he was still alive! Rushing to the local magistrate's house to report this, they found that plump official about to tuck into his dinner. When they pleaded that their son was still alive and begged him to go and cut him down from the gallows, the magistrate is reputed to have laughed and retorted that their son was no more alive than the two chickens on his plate that he was about to eat.

At this point the plucked and roasted chickens – a rooster and a hen – on his platter stood up and began to crow. The chastened magistrate rushed back to the gallows and cut the poor young man down. He was given a full pardon, his miraculous escape from death being attributed to Santo Domingo. Since then, not only does the town have a rooster and a hen on its coat of arms, but the cathedral itself has a chicken coop inside it, at the back of the church, which contains two (live) chickens.

It was very interesting when we visited Portugal a month later to discover a similar story of a pilgrim wrongfully accused of theft in the town of Barcellos. This unjustly condemned pilgrim too was saved in like manner by miraculous intervention – but in this case the miracle is attributed to SanTiago himself. The Barcellos cockerel is now part of Portuguese folklore.

In ancient times, when pilgrims could take one of several routes through Spain to Santiago de Compostela, spreading the story that such a miracle had taken place in Santo Domnigo de la Calzada would certainly have helped to draw these amazed foreign visitors into the town (and so ensure a steady stream of customers for the local innkeepers and merchants). Which pilgrim would not have chosen a stopover in this town, where he could hear the story 'first hand', visit the place where the miracle took place – and even see the chicken coop in the cathedral where resided, if not the actual birds that rose from the dead, at least their descendants?

Having arrived early at the hostel, I visited a museum called The Camino Experience, which displayed the history of the Camino and also showed a documentary about the miracle story of the chickens who rose from the dead. From the local supermarket I got some food so we could have a late lunch in the sunny courtyard of our hostel, and then went up to our bunks for a short rest. Walking out later to explore the town I chanced upon a small bookshop where I bought some postcards and a copy of Mario Vargas Llosa's *Cartas a un joven novelista* for my daughter, who was studying Spanish at university – and then Shivantha and I ended up in the cathedral where we attended the choral mass at 8 pm. The singing was beautiful – and it was gratifying to me that with my rapidly improving Spanish I could follow the Spanish service.

Tuesday 3rd May 2011: Santo Domingo de Calzada to Belorado

We left the *albergue* at 7.45 am, having breakfasted on the apples, cheese, bread and juice I'd bought yesterday. One of the pilgrims who had stayed the night there with us had left a bag of food which was too much for him or her to carry on – pears, cakes, a tin of mussels – so we decided to take it with us. We made reasonable time, reaching Villoria de Rioja across the border in the autonomous region of Leon y Castille, and since it was only 1.30 in the afternoon, we decided to press on to Belorado 8 km away. Prudently we got Fadi to phone ahead and book us a place at the Albergue Cuatro Cantones.

I was the first to arrive, ahead of my son, and made good conversation in Spanish with the lady at the reception desk. Having showered off the dirt of the road, we were able to give our clothes to the proprietor, Nicholas, to wash and dry. This was a comfortable, clean, family-run place with a small swimming pool and patio to sit on outside – but unfortunately it was drizzling in the afternoon, so we could not avail ourselves of the opportunity of even sitting outside, let alone having a dip in the pool.

Dinner was provided for all those staying there by the family who ran the *albergue* – the typical pilgrim menu, not for a fixed price, but with an option to "pay what you think the dinner was worth". The place is well maintained by the family – Nicholas (who reminded me of an older version of former Australian cricket captain Ricky Ponting!), his son Iker and daughter-in-law Jana.

Wednesday 4th May 2011: Belorado to San Juan de Ortega

Having left the *albergue* at Belorado by 8.15 after a breakfast of bread, butter, jam, cake and coffee we made good time, stopping after 8 km at a bar in Espinosa del Camino for coffee and at Villafranca de Montes de Oca for lunch (garlic mushrooms, garlic sardines and Limon beer) before we undertook the 12 km stretch to our destination of San Juan de Ortega.

One of the pleasures of doing this journey on foot over many days is the opportunity of stopping at quaint out-of-the-way places for a sip and a bite – and sampling the everyday foods that the local folk eat. To me, travelling overseas does not simply mean getting into a plane and arriving in some big city, and then staying in a five star hotel that is like any other five star hotel in the world, eating the same ubiquitous five star meals that one finds in such places. I once heard a British couple seated at the table next to us in a hotel in Myanmar (Burma) complaining loudly that they were not being served decent bacon, eggs and toast for breakfast. I could not help thinking to myself at the time, what is the purpose of travelling halfway around the world to eat the same type of food that you can eat every day at home?

The Villafranca de Montes de Oca at which we had lunch is one of many *Villafrancas* (Town of the Franks) along the Camino – so named because they were home to the many Franks (French) who came as pilgrims and then settled down to stay on as artisans and craftsmen. Montes de Oca may be translated as 'mountains of the wild geese' – this was once a wild unpopulated area notorious for the bandits who used to prey on travelling pilgrims.

Along the way to San Juan de Ortega we passed a poignant memorial *El Monumento de los Caidos* (The Monument to the Fallen) built at the site where Franco's troops massacred some 300 people. The stark memorial is surmounted by Picasso's famous *Dove* – the line drawing he made with just three brush-strokes.

San Juan has been one of the classic pilgrim halts along the Camino for centuries, and has a historic parish hostel made even more famous by the former parish priest Jose Maria who had lived here for many years and died in 2008. His legendary bread and garlic soup has fed innumerable pilgrims who stayed at the *albergue* over the years.

We had decided to stay here at the local *casa rural*, so our friend Fadi had kindly phoned ahead and booked us a room in the names of 'Shiv and his father from Sri Lanka'. When I walked into the place some minutes ahead of my son and informed the man at reception, *"Hemos reservado una habitación para Shiv y su padre de Sri Lanka"* ("We have a reservation for a room for Shiv and his father of Sri Lanka"), he looked up from his register in surprise and asked me, a grey bearded stranger, *"Donde es tu padre?"* ("Where is your father?")

Shivantha soon walked in with Fadi and we all had a good laugh. We then checked into the comfortable *casa rural* La Henera where we were given a clean room with two beds and attached bath. I had a long warm shower – we had walked 24 km that day – and washed and hung out my clothes. This lovely little village is home to no more than 30 people. It is the influx of pilgrims throughout the year that keeps the local economy going.

Ortega is Spanish for 'nettle' – and nettles must have abounded in this wild and isolated place at the time San Juan (a great builder of bridges, churches and pilgrim hospices, just like his mentor Santo Domingo) founded an Augustinian monastery here in 1150. The chapel he built is dedicated to San Nicolas de Barri, and is situated in the village square next to the parish hostel.

In time, the village developed a beautiful church and a monastery full of monks – and a regular influx of pilgrims who found this place an oasis within the scrub forests of Burgos province. By the late 17th century, however, the place ran out of money and devotees – and the abandoned church with its huge ceilings and cavernous stone niches was used by the local farmers as a place to store their hay. Until the middle of the 20th century, the only inhabitants of this place were a few families of farmers.

Fortunately for the village, the local priest Father Jose Maria took it upon himself in the 1960s to resurrect the village. Until his death he personally presided over San Juan's rescue and rehabilitation. The old monastery has now been converted into a pilgrim hostel, and with help from the federal government the church and its sculptures are being preserved. The fact that the church spent a couple of hundred years full of hay was fortuitous because as a result the statues and sculptures were protected from the elements.

The capitals of the pillars in this chapel have some fascinating old sculptures, particularly of the Nativity and the Annunciation. It is here that the *Milagro de la Luz* (Miracle of the Light) is said to take place on the days of the spring and autumn equinoxes. Between 5 and 7 pm on these days, the rays of the setting sun enter through the window and illuminate the sculpture of the Virgin Mary in the scene of the Annunciation. In the crypt itself is a beautiful sepulchre bearing an effigy of San Juan, with some delicate tracery stonework.

Having explored the chapel and the interesting 16th century courtyard of the pilgrim hostel, we sat for a while in the village square with our glasses of wine, just enjoying the late afternoon sun and these leisurely moments - '*Il dolce far niente*' as the Italians say, the 'sweetness of doing nothing' - until the others came to call us for dinner. Shivantha and I sat at a table at the Bar Marcela with two Dutch men – one a retired police sergeant, the other a retired professor of public administration.

Why, I asked them during the course of our conversation, were they walking the Camino? The professor told us that he had been teaching for many years and had just retired because he found that working part-time was not financially feasible. He now had to decide what to do with the rest of his life, which he estimates will stretch for another 30 years or so – being 65 and knowing that his father had lived to 94 – and he felt that the atmosphere and solitude of the Camino might provide him with the opportunity of making that decision.

The sergeant had walked the Camino ten years before – and now that he is 45, the age at which his own father had died unexpectedly of a heart attack, he decided to undertake the journey again to spend time thinking about his father – and reflecting.

"I had the same relationship with my father that many boys of that era did," he reflected. "I respected him, I looked on him as my idol, and wanted to be like him when I grew up – but I cannot remember him ever telling me that he loved me, nor did I ever get the opportunity to let him know how much I loved him. Men did not express such thoughts to their children. One day I was brought home from school early because he had dropped dead at work from a massive heart attack. I could not even say goodbye to him. I was only 15 – and I was devastated.

"On the Camino this time, I think about him, and even talk to him. Wherever he is now, he will know how much he means to me."

He looked at me – and then at Shivantha. "You are very fortunate that you both have this opportunity of walking the Camino together as father and son."

It is no longer a surprise to me on this journey how we meet complete strangers and, during the short time that our paths coincide, share such intimate thoughts – matters we would not talk about with our near and dear ones at home. There are times when all of us need someone we can talk to – and it must be easier with someone who doesn't know us too well. We can open the thoughts of our hearts to them because we recognise kindred spirits as we share this journey on the Camino.

It was good spending time chatting with these two men. This evening meal that we shared was just a brief encounter with anonymous humans we had not met before and are unlikely to meet again. We were discovering for ourselves that there is a bond between pilgrims along the Camino – and I believe this bond is based on mutual respect. It requires a certain personal quality to set oneself a challenge such as this, and we found that the nature of the folk we met during our journey reflected those common qualities of courage and humility.

People walk the Camino for many reasons – but there are some common themes. Walking the Camino provides an opportunity of taking time off the mundane activities of a householder and being granted the space to think, to remember, to get to know oneself – and to reflect on the memory of loved ones.

This evening we had met the Dutch police sergeant who was walking the Camino in memory of his dead father, and previously we had hiked in the company of the Australian mother who was walking the Camino after the tragic death of her son. Shivantha and I felt humbly grateful that the two of us were having the privilege in our own lifetimes of doing this special pilgrimage together.

Thursday 5th May 2011: San Juan de Ortega to Burgos

We had decided this morning to take our time about leaving San Juan de Ortega, so while Shivantha slept, I sat at his computer and worked on an article to send to a magazine back home. It was about 9.30 by the time we left; we walked at a relaxed pace along a delightful path that passed through oak and pine woods.

About half an hour after we left San Juan de Ortega, we passed *El Puente Canto* - the Bridge of Song, a simple stone bridge said to have been built by San Juan himself. It stands peacefully in a sunlit meadow with the river Vena, here no more than a little brook, babbling underneath. I remarked to Shivantha that I had noticed at this stage, two weeks into our journey, that I was able to walk relatively fast with less breathlessness going up slopes compared to our first week on the Camino. This pilgrimage was making us fit.

Today's hike took us through Atapuerca - the site of archaeological excavations that, going on since 1978, have revealed the remains of what were almost certainly the earliest human beings in Europe: *Homo antecessor*. The Visitor Information Centre of Atapuerca, situated about 500 metres from the main road, was disappointing - just a few large posters with a lot of prose and few pictures, with not even a canteen where we could get something to eat or drink. It was not the reward we expected after detouring off the main path in the hot sun to visit the place.

The visitor centre we discovered was just an office from where trips could be arranged to the ancient limestone caves some 3 km away where the fossils were found. The caves have been designated a UNESCO World Heritage site, and with archaeologists still excavating there, are reputed to contain a rich fossil record of pre-historic human activity in these parts that goes back almost a million years.

About 2 km beyond Atapuerca we reached, after a somewhat steep rocky path, *El Cruceiro* (The Cross). At 1,080 metres above sea level this was the high point of today's walk. From here we had our first view of the city of Burgos - but had to remind ourselves that it was still a good four hours' walk away!

During today's 4½-hour walk that covered 17 km, we had stopped periodically - at Agues, Atapuerca and Orbaneja - for food and drink, and made it to Villafria, one of the industrial suburbs of Burgos, by half past four in the afternoon. Here were quite a few hotels with interesting names – Hotel Buenos Aires, Hotel Las Vegas, etc – but we opted for the simpler Hotel Irunako, paying €40 for *habitacion doble con dos camas y bain* (double room with two beds and attached bathroom).

After settling into our room, Shivantha got on the internet to sort out his rent payment and other mundane matters in New York while I went downstairs to the bar and had a peaceful glass of wine seated out in the evening sun. When my son, his financial transactions done, came down, we tucked into some tasty Pinxhos for our evening meal.

Friday 6th May 2011: Burgos

We decided that today was going to be a day of rest and relaxation *(una dia para descansar)* which we would make use of to explore and enjoy Burgos. Shivantha was tired and slept while I worked on a couple of articles to be sent to *Australian Doctor* magazine back home – an opinion piece and a travel article. We left in time to take the noon bus into the city, stopping off to visit the military museum (*Museo Regional Militair*) -- a fascinating place with its collections of model soldiers, ancient weapons and historic uniforms. There was a large sign in each of the rooms advising visitors that taking photographs was forbidden. I discovered in the military medicine section some impressive uniforms and coats of arms which I was very keen to capture on film. On an impulse, I went up to the uniformed guard in the room, introduced myself as a member of *'Ejercito de Australie'* (the Australian Army), showed him my identity card and asked politely if I may have his permission to take a photograph of these items. He scrutinised my identity card, asked me to wait, and a short time later returned with two men in Spanish military uniforms, who turned out to be the officer in charge of the museum and his assistant. The men were pleased to talk with me – as I was with them – and reassured me that I could take whatever photographs I wanted to in that room.

From the museum we walked to the city centre, stopping to admire the statue of El Cid and having a bite to eat (in two different bars!) before visiting the amazing Burgos Cathedral.

I can spend hours in places like museums and cathedrals, taking my time to look at everything on display and diligently reading all the notices and descriptions. Fortunately, Shivantha also shares this trait – perhaps it is not just the colour of our eyes and the shape of our nose that parents pass on in our genes – so we spent a very fulfilling day in the museum and cathedral.

The imposing Cathedral of Santa Maria in Burgos is an outstanding example of Gothic architecture, very French in its outward appearance. Inside we found beautiful collections of artworks and sculptures, some grand cloisters and a splendid cupola.

By the time we had finished it was almost six, so we stopped at a *Farmacia* to get some antihistamine cream for my bedbug bites and got the No. 8 bus back to our hotel. We had seen two good sights today, the military museum and the cathedral, so we had a pilgrim dinner at the Hotel and turned in early.

Saturday 7th May 2011: Burgos to Rabe de Calzados

Due to an unexpected shower of rain it was 9.20 by the time we left the Hotel Irunako after breakfast, planning to catch the 9.30 bus into the city. I had not made allowance for the fact that it was Saturday and the buses only ran on the hour rather than half-hourly, so it was 10.00 by the time we got on the bus to the city centre. We decided to visit the Museum of Human Evolution which is based on the Atapuerca findings and *Homo antecessor* – and spent a couple of absorbing hours there. Unlike the Visitor Information Centre, this place was both informative and interesting. We took our time – we were learning that on the Camino that there was no rush to finish and no deadline to meet. If it was too late to start walking, we would just find another place to stay for the night and leave the following day on our Camino.

After we had had our fill at the museum we walked to the bus station only to find that the next bus to Castrojeriz was scheduled for Monday evening! So, after a forgettable *menu de dia* lunch at Cafe Salamanca near the bus station, we decided to start walking.

We passed the Burgos Military Hospital and decided to detour off the main Camino, which passes through the El Parral park, in order to visit the *Monasterio de Santa María la Real de Las Huelgas*, the royal convent of Cistercian nuns. The abbess of this convent was also given the responsibility of running the nearby King's Hospice (*El Hospital del Rey)*. Founded in 1195 by King Alfonso VIII (whose wife, Eleanor was the sister of England's crusader king Richard the Lionheart, being the daughter of the Plantaganet King Henry II and Queen Eleanor of Aquitaine), *El Hospital del Rey* enjoyed royal patronage and was a great shelter for pilgrims along the Camino. Today its buildings house the Law Faculty of the University of Burgos.

In days gone by pilgrims to Santiago who wished to stay at the Royal Hospice had to show their *Credencials*, signed by the bishop of their diocese to identify them as genuine pilgrims – and on their homeward journey they had to show their *Compostela*. If their documents were in order, they were entitled to stay here for two nights, being looked after by knights of the Cistercian order and given rations consisting of 20 ounces of bread, 12 ounces of meat and 16 ounces of red wine. For a couple of days at least, the footsore and penniless pilgrim could enjoy the hospitality of the King.

The Royal Abbey of Las Huelgas (the Spanish word *monasterio* really translates as 'abbey', which includes both monasteries for monks as well as convents for nuns) is about 600 metres off the main Camino, but is well worth a visit. Inside its rectangular Chapel of St James built in Moorish style is an unusual 13th century statue of the saint dressed in a colourful tunic. What is curious about this particular statue is that its right arm is designed to move. It is believed that the statue was used in initiation ceremonies of the Cistercian order. When new knights were initiated, they were dubbed on their shoulders by no less a person than the saint (or at least his statue) himself.

Walking onwards at a brisk pace we reached Rabe de las Calzados shortly before 6 pm, and checked into the Albergue Liberanos Domine where Fadi and the others were staying. After a meal of olives, tortilla and soft drinks topped off with a *chupito* of Panxera, I examined Fadi's back. Clinically his problem appeared to be sprained back muscles rather than a slipped disc. I advised him to apply some heat-generating ointment, take anti-inflammatory medication – and have his backpack transported instead of carrying it himself.

Today marks 20 days since we were in St Jean Pied de Port – and we have now completed 300 km of our journey. It was a good time to reflect on what we had learned so far along our journey. What I was beginning to appreciate about life on the Camino was *Time*. For the past three weeks we had enjoyed having Time – to think and to breathe, to talk and to ponder, to explore and perhaps even to grow. I was being given the pleasure and privilege of Time to share food and wine – and moments and views – with my son.

I realised that I was having Time to give thanks for what I have, to identify what I don't have and whether I need to have them, and to work on what I really need to have.

Sunday 8th May 2011: Rabe de la Calzada to Hontanas

After the usual breakfast of coffee, bread, butter, jam and Marie biscuits at the *albergue*, we left around 8.15 and did a steady walk across the *meseta* through Hornillas del Camino and San Bol to reach Hontanas, where around 2 pm we checked into the Albergue El Pundito – a pleasant place where we had a twin room for €22. Having carried our packs up to our room we came down to the dining room and had a good meal: *Olla San Anton* (a traditional stew containing chickpeas, sausage and various parts of the pig including 'pig's tail, pig's jowls and pig's ears'), fish in sauce, dessert of *arroz con leche* and two bottles of wine between us. We followed this with coffee in the street just outside the *albergue*. It was a good opportunity to just relax and talk after our five-hour walk.

This whole journey, in fact, is an opportunity for me and my son – the curly-haired infant I used to carry, the mischievous little boy who used to sit astride my shoulders and order me to run, pretending he was riding a horse (and sometimes even an elephant!) to get to know each other as adults. Here we were thousands of kilometres from home, a grey-bearded man of sixty and a young man exactly half that age whose hairline was just starting to recede and whose jet-black beard was just beginning to show the occasional grey hair, making this 800 km journey on foot to the Field of Stars.

And as we shared this journey and I got to know this young man, I was coming to the realisation that were he not my son, he is someone I would certainly have chosen as my friend.

Khalil Gibran said in his poem *On Children*, 'We can give them their bodies but not their minds'. Although my son is his own person and is in many ways different to me in his outlook and ideas, yet he is also a human being with whom I have a lot in common, probably more than with anyone else – except perhaps my own father.

Chapter 8: Dinner by Candlelight

Monday 9th May 2011: Hontanas to Puente Itero

We were up early and, having had coffee and *napolitanas* from the *albergue* bar plus the apples and yoghurt that I'd bought yesterday, managed to set off by 7.15. Along the way we passed the splendid ruins of an ancient abbey, the monastery and hospice of San Anton Abad – the patron saint of domestic animals, an Egyptian monastic who is often depicted in paintings with a pig at his feet.

We walked briskly and were at the entrance to the town of Castrojeriz about 90 minutes after we left Hontanas. We had a coffee there with two Italians, Mario and Ruggero, with whom Shivantha conversed fluently in Italian, and then went across to see the *Iglesia Maria de Manzanas* (Church of St Mary of the Apples). It was barred and locked, so we disappointedly turned around and were about to leave through the courtyard gate when a young Italian couple came in and went up to the door of the church. When I spoke to them, they said the priest was coming in ten minutes to open it for them. As a result we had the fortunate opportunity of entering the church with them and admiring its delightful rose window as well a magnificent statue of Santiago in full pilgrim regalia.

We walked on and had quite a steep climb to Alto Mostelares, for the last part of which Shivantha once again carried my pack in addition to his own. The view from up here was fabulous.

Ruggero had told us, while we were having coffee, about a special *albergue* further on at Puente Itero, just before the bridge across the river Pisuerga. It was run by an Italian confraternity, he said, and he was planning to stay the night there himself. Reaching there around 1 pm and seeing Ruggero seated on the bench outside the *albergue* which was closed, we decided to stay there ourselves. I sat with Ruggero and we chatted utilising Italian, Spanish, English and our phrase books, while Shivantha walked the 1.5 km to the next village, Itero de la Vega, to bring *bocadillos*, fruit, yoghurt and a bottle of wine for our lunch. We shared the wine with Ruggero, Mario (who passed by) and two of the *hospitaleros*, Bruno and Franco, who arrived a short while later to open up the *albergue* and prepare for the arrival of pilgrims.

Our stay at this unique *albergue* – three weeks into our pilgrimage on the Camino – was surely one of the best days of our journey

The *albergue* of San Nicolas, manned by three to four *hospitaleros*, is situated at Puente Itero in a 10th century building which was recently restored by the Perrugia-based Confraternity of St James *(Confraternita di San Jacopo di Compostella)*. It is located where a 12th century pilgrim hospice once stood. The building consists of a single long hall with a small chapel at one end and a set of five double bunk beds at the other end – with a long dining table in the middle.

What was so special for us about this *albergue* was not its location but the exemplary spirit of service shown by the *hospitaleros* who run the place. All the other places at which we stayed during our Camino were essentially run as commercial establishments, providing cheap accommodation and food for pilgrims walking The Way, but in a manner and at a price designed to earn a living for those running these establishments.

San Nicolas however was different.

Here we did not have to pay a fee on arrival. We were welcomed, and when we asked about payment we were told that we could make a donation (*donativo*) when we left the following morning.

The *albergue* itself has no electricity. Lighting is entirely by candles and cooking is done on a gas stove. Behind the main *albergue* is a garden in which there is a small building housing toilets and showers – fortunately provided with electric lights and hot water. In order to draw water from the nearby well for the purpose of washing clothes there is a quaint and creaky hand-operated pump – which brought back memories of the one we had in the large garden at *Lakmahal*, used every day by the gardener (*thottakkaran*) to water the plants.

The *hospitaleros* here provide pilgrims with a cooked dinner. We were treated to salad, pasta, chorizo and cake, but before dinner, we were privileged to participate in a ceremony, unique among all the *albergues* in which we stayed – and one which epitomised the humility and sense of dedication which these *hospitaleros* bring to their task of caring for pilgrims.

At 7.30 in the evening, all 12 of us pilgrims staying at the *albergue* were asked to be seated in a semicircle in the chapel. Our hosts were all wearing their scallop shell-covered black capes. One by one we submitted ourselves to the ceremony. Each of us was asked in turn to place one foot in a bowl held by a *hospitalero* – and while another *hospitalero* read a prayer of blessing, a third poured water from a special pitcher on to our feet and washed it. After drying the foot with a towel, the *hospitalero* kissed the foot. This was certainly a demonstration of the true humility with which these special men accepted their calling.

Following the ceremony of washing our feet, we were asked to sit down at the long table – by candlelight – and served dinner.

Our offer to help with serving and clearing up were gently declined – "No, you pilgrims are tired after your long journey. You sit and allow us to serve you" – and we felt a genuine sense of fellowship with our fellow pilgrims, making conversation in a mixture of Italian, French, Spanish and English.

Roland, who had walked all the way from Lyon with his pet donkey Praline and was planning to get to Santiago for his 65th birthday on June 10th was telling Shivantha about his journey, while Ruggero from Trento in Italy, Michelle from Toronto in Canada and I were engaged in a most entertaining trilingual conversation.

After dinner all of us sat on the wooden benches outside the *albergue*. The sun was going down and soon the glow of the setting sun caressed the landscape. In time darkness fell, the moon came out – and after a while we could see above us a spectacular night sky. Far from the pollution and smog of the big city, the stars and constellations were so clear. In medieval times people believed that the sky above their heads was a barrier – a semi-permeable membrane if you will – that literally separated us humans down below from God and his people up in heaven. Given the vista of the sky as we had here, it was not difficult to empathise with such a view.

Shivantha and Ruggero had found a guitar somewhere inside the *albergue* and sang for us as we sat outside – after which each of us was encouraged to sing a song in our own language. A couple of the Dutch ladies even danced to one of Shivantha's songs. Sharing this experience of pilgrimage so far from home created a unique spirit of conviviality among this group of beings – outwardly so different yet inwardly so connected.

It was certainly an evening to remember. All of us who came to this place as strangers came to realise the simple yet profound truth: that there is much more in this world that we have in common than that which divides us.

Tuesday 10th May 2011: Puente Itero to Poblacion de Campos

After breakfast and effusive farewells to the *hospitaleros* we left San Nicolas. We who had come to this *albergue* the previous day as individuals on the Camino, were leaving the place the next morning as friends – and in truth, as members of that great family of pilgrims on the Camino.

Shivantha walked with Roland, having an interesting conversation with him in French while I had Dennis, an American geologist from Boulder, Colorado for company. Roland had served a couple of years in the French Marines, then become a chef and worked in various places including the prestigious Eiffel Tower restaurant. He had two sons, he told us. One is now working as a chef himself, but the younger boy had died last year at the age of 17 of leukaemia. Roland had set out to walk all the way to Santiago from his home in Lyons in France, a distance of over a thousand kilometres, with his donkey Praline. Some nights he would camp out in the open while at other times he would stay in *albergues*. He had an intriguing pennant on his staff – depicting an eagle, a lion and two stars. The eagle, he explained, represented his family name Garin, the lion was for his city Lyons, while the two stars were for his two sons.

We stopped for coffee in Boadilla and for lunch in in the town of Fromista with its UNESCO World Heritage church. San Martin in Fromista is one of the most famous Romanesque churches in the world and is associated with the Knights Templar, that mysterious order of Christian soldier monks who were ruthlessly wiped out, with the connivance of a weak Pope Clement V, by the French King Phillip IV on Friday the 13th of October 1307.

Here Denis left us to take a bus to Leon. We left town and had walked for about half a kilometre in the hot sun along the N-611A when luckily we were stopped by a lady in a car who, recognising the scallop shells on our hats which denoted us as pilgrims, pointed us in the correct direction – back through the town!

We made it to Poblacion de Campos, about 5½ hours and 20 km since we left San Nicolas, and decided to stop as the sun was hot. We booked into the Hostal Amanecer en Campos – €45 with breakfast and Wi-Fi – and after the usual shower, washing of clothes and rest, we walked to a bar near our accommodation and had our evening meal of tins of sardines, calamari and mussels along with a bottle of olives and a €7 bottle of very acceptable wine.

Wednesday 11th May 2011: Poblacion de Campos to Carrion de Los Condes

We took our time leaving the hostel as we were able to use Shivantha's computer with the hostel's Wi-Fi connection to talk to Chitra on Skype. It was the first time my wife saw me with my grey beard and her comment to Shivantha was, "Your father looks awful!" Although I did not tell her so, I must admit that I could not help agreeing with her.

We left, having thanked the *hospitalera* Imna who had washed our clothes and been very helpful to us, and walked along the Senda, the pilgrim path that runs parallel to the main road, through Villarmentero and Villalcazar. Along the way we met a man walking along the path towards us, carrying a large red umbrella and wearing a white T-shirt with the word 'PEACE' in several languages. We stopped to speak to him and discovered he was from the French Indian Ocean island of Réunion, on his way back to Paris from Santiago where he had gone to seek help for his daughter – who he told us was suffering from a mental illness. From the symptoms he described, she seemed to be having a psychotic condition which was proving non-responsive to medical treatment.

Our meeting this man led to Shivantha and me talking, as we walked, about the problem of mental illness. Even in this 21st century, the therapies available to treat mental illness – conditions like depression, bipolar disorder or schizophrenia – are not always effective. Medical science has learned over the centuries how to kill germs and repair damaged bodies, and we can treat infection and trauma very effectively. But how do you treat someone who is considered mad by the standards of society – and does not realise they are mad? How do you treat someone who suffers from depression, yet refuses to acknowledge that they are ill and accept therapy – when in any case the convincingly promoted 'antidepressant' medications made by pharmaceutical companies are ineffective in some people and have unacceptable side effects in a small percentage of patients who take them?

This word 'antidepressant' is a wonderful name from the point of view of the companies that manufacture these drugs – it sounds so efficacious, giving the impression that all anyone who has depression has to do is to keep taking these tablets and all will be well. In reality, this class of drugs – Selective Serotonin Re-uptake Inhibitors (SSRIs) and Serotonin and Noradrenaline Re-uptake Inhibitors (SNRIs) – reduce the re-uptake of certain chemicals in the nervous system and by thus affecting chemical messengers in the brain can modify how the brain responds to certain messages. Their exact mechanism of action is still unknown. They can certainly help in treating depression in many people – but their use has to be as an adjunct to other forms of therapy such as psychotherapy and cognitive behavioural therapy, rather than as a panacea for all patients suffering from depression.

We talked and walked – and stopped beside a metal sculpture of a pilgrim at a place called Revenga to have a drink. Lunch was at Villalcazar (healthy *raciones* of chicken, fish, calamari and mushrooms). The food was good and we ate far too much –

which meant we had to rest for a while to allow the food to leave our stomachs. We finally left and after another 5 km reached Carrion de los Condes by 3 pm.

We checked into the 13th century Monasterio de Santa Clara, where it is said that St Francis of Assisi stayed when he walked the Camino. The dormitory was full, but we were able to get one of the individual rooms for €42. After our customary shower and clean-up we walked into the town for a drink – Aquarius Limon, a non-fizzy soft drink which is quite refreshing and of which we have both become great fans along this journey.

We met the three Dutch ladies with whom we had stayed last night at San Nicolas and stopped to have a chat with them as well as with the owner of the local Renault garage, a friendly Spanish man who spoke English with a French accent. It transpired that he had grown up in France, where his parents had fled during the time of Franco. We chatted with him – me in English and Shivantha in French – and then left to find an optometrist to fix my glasses, because while we were walking this morning the screw had fallen off the hinge holding the arm to the frame. At a shop called Optica, the kind optometrist fixed it for me and refused any payment, smilingly shaking her head and wishing us both "Buon Camino" when I asked her how much I owed her. It was another instance along the Camino when we have experienced the kindness of strangers.

We decided to get some food from the local *supermercado* for our dinner, which we ate with great enjoyment in our room – olives, mussels, calamari, garlic toast, yoghurt and a bottle of Campo Viejo Rioja wine.

Throughout our journey, Shivantha had been carrying his laptop computer in his pack, and was keen to show me, an avowed technophobe, the many benefits he had as a result. He was able to talk with his girlfriend in Italy and his mother in Melbourne, attend to banking matters in New York, listen to music from the vast store in his iPod – and even download music and movies from the Internet. He had offered to download any movie that I wanted to see – and tonight, encouraged by his recommendation of the Ridley Scott movie *Kingdom of Heaven*, I suggested he purchase it for us to watch.

So it was that in a guest room in the Convento de Santa Clara in the small Spanish town of Carrion de los Condes, father and son sat together, shared the rest of the bottle of Rioja wine – and watched the story of Balin of Ibelin, the blacksmith's son who went to the Crusades.

Thursday 12th May 2011: Carrion de Los Condes to Terradillos de los Templarios

Leaving the convent by 7.30 am we had a coffee at the bar 50 metres down the road and then, passing the San Zoilo monastery which is now a luxury hotel, got on to the old Roman road known as the Via Aquitana.

This 2,000-year-old road is as straight as they come – in characteristic Roman Empire fashion it represents the shortest route from A to B. It passed through featureless landscapes and monotonous fields of wheat for about 16 km until, all of a sudden it seemed, we came upon the small town of Calzadilla de la Cueza.

We had kept walking through the endless wheat fields, thinking that the town would never appear – and then suddenly out of nowhere there it was, tucked away in a hollow on an incline. Who should we meet here but Fadi and Julia, seated outside the bar on the main street (as in many of these villages, the Camino passes along the main street of the village). We had a drink and bite (artichokes and sardines) with them, and bought two new *Credencials* for €2 each from the owner of the bar, Cesar Acero, who is himself a seasoned Camino walker. Like so many others we have met along The Way, he too (despite having walked the Camino several times over many years) was seeing pilgrims from Sri Lanka for the first time.

We continued on our way for another 9 km to Terradillos de los Templarios, where we got a room in the new Los Templarios *albergue*. Having replenished our fluids, washed our clothes and had the pilgrim menu for dinner, we watched the rest of *Kingdom of Heaven* – a movie set in the 12th century during the time of fierce battles between Christians and Moslems for the control of Jerusalem.

It is a great story with much that is relevant for us in the present day.

Friday 13th May: Terradillos de los Templarios to Sahagun

Interestingly, today is Friday the 13th and we are in Terradillos de los Templarios, a village long associated with the Knights Templar, whose churches we had come across previously in places like Eunate and Fromista. The superstition about Friday the 13th being unlucky is said to be associated with Friday 13th October 1307, when the French King Philippe IV, with the collusion of Pope Clement V, swooped on the Order of the Knights Templar. The Knights, originally an order of soldier monks among whose tasks was providing protection for pilgrims along the Camino, had become a powerful organisation both financially and politically, and were seen as a threat to both church and state. Many members of the order, including the Grand Master Jacques de Molay, were arrested at dawn on 13th October 1307, tortured and put to death – and the order, which in modern language could really be described as a supranational NGO, was wiped out.

Having slept in that morning we had a leisurely breakfast and commenced walking around 10 am. We took this stretch easy, passing through Moratinos and San Nicolas del Real Camino, and used Shivantha's mobile phone to make a reservation at Hostal Escachar in Sahagun. I managed to perform this task speaking entirely in Spanish ("*Soimos peregrinos – quiremos una habatacion doble con bain*") and felt quite pleased with myself.

Reaching the Hostal in Sahagun around two, we showered and washed our clothes (including my hat) and laid them out to dry in the bright sunshine. Afterwards we walked to the Restaurante Luis in the nearby Plaza Major and had a pilgrim meal. I ordered *Sopa Castellana* (called Garlic Soup but which is really a soup made with pig fat and just a hint of garlic!) followed by calamari fried in garlic. Returning to the hotel, Shivantha went up to the room to rest while I, now quite confident with my command of Spanish, stopped to have a chat with the hotel owner with whom I shared a *chupito* (small shot glass) of *Panxhera* – the equivalent of Italian grappa.

We rested for about an hour and then went for a walk in the town, which in ancient times was a seat of great ecclesiastical power. It still has some fabulous buildings dating back to Roman times and the Baroque period. We saw the impressive Arco de San Benito, part of the ruins of the San Benito monastery which at one time was one of the most powerful in Spain. Nearby was the chapel of the Convento de Santa Clara, and since they were commencing vespers at the time we walked in, both of us sat through the service and were rewarded with a pilgrim blessing.

Returning through the Plaza Mayor after getting some food from the supermarket we met Julia and Fadi, who had information about train timetables as they were planning to travel by train to Leon tomorrow. Shivantha and I discussed this possibility – Sahagun represents the halfway mark of our Camino – and decided that we too would make our journey from Sahagun to Leon by train.

Chapter 9. The Train in Spain

Saturday 14th May 2011: Sahagun to Leon

Having got up early we got on to the internet to book a hotel in Leon, and managed to get a double room for €50 at a place called Padre Isla. We walked to Cafe Ruta to have *cafe y panrico* (coffee and cake – literally 'rich bread') for breakfast, and then while Shivantha went back to the room to rest, I walked over to have a look at the Convent Museum. A nun who must have been no more than four feet tall showed me round. Here was an unusual statue of the Virgin Mary adorned as a pilgrim – setting an example to devotees to follow her to St James' shrine. To me it was yet another example of how the church makes use of graven images and implausible allegories to keep the gullible masses faithful.

Also in this museum was the sarcophagus of one of the great warrior kings of Europe, King Alfonso VI – Alfonso the Valiant - and that of four of his five wives. The fourth wife, I learned, was a Moslem princess Zaida of Seville, who converted to Christianity, took the name Isabel, and was the mother of his only son. At the end of the commentary – which although entirely in Spanish I was able to follow and found quite interesting – the nun asked me for a "*donativo*", which I felt was fair recompense for her trouble.

After getting our *Credencials* stamped at the Iglesia San Tirso we had lunch – paella for me and pizza for Shivantha – and then walked to the Sahagun railway station to take the train to Leon. The 54 km trip which would have taken us three days of walking took only 40 minutes by train! We walked from the railway station in Leon to the hotel I'd booked, to find Leonie, Claire, Fadi and Julia had all made reservations at the same place. It was intriguing how throughout this Camino the six of us have come together at various places.

After a lunch of tinned olives, octopus and pimentos we went exploring this 'gorgeous sandstone capital of Castille', first inside the very interesting Museo de Leon and then outside the city's elegant Gothic cathedral on the Plaza de la Regal. In the evening we met up with the others at the Plaza San Martin, the 'happening place' of Leon. Outside the Plaza's colourful restaurants we sat at rustic wooden tables on rough wooden benches, with myriads of others – pilgrims as well as locals – enjoying Castilian tapas and wine. As Shivantha observed, "Walking the Camino is a wonderful opportunity to make new friendships, gain some knowledge, enjoy good food – and imbibe a lot of great wine in congenial company."

Sunday 15th May 2011: Leon to Virgen del Camino

I was up early as usual, so showered and left the room by eight to have a coffee – and had to walk for over half an hour, it being Sunday in Spain, to find a place that was open. Shivantha was still sleeping when I got back, so I too decided to sleep in (after all, it *was* Sunday!) and around ten we left to have a good look around the cathedral, which dates from the 13th century and is renowned for its splendid stained glass windows. Numbering over 100, these windows in effect invite sunlight into the church, refracting this rainbow of colours all over the interior and making it, in marked contrast to the all the dark and gloomy *iglesias* we had seen up to now, one of the brightest churches along the Camino.

We spent a few quiet moments inside the small chapel marked 'Enter only for praying' and then left to visit the Basilica of San Isidore with its fascinating museum and pantheon.

This Basilica (also called the Royal Collegiate Church of St Isidore) houses the relics of San Isidoro of Seville who lived in pre-Islamic Spain from 560 to 636 AD. He was Archbishop of Seville for 30 years and one of Spain's greatest scholars. The first known encyclopaedia in the western world, *Etymologiae*, was written by him.

Inside the Royal Pantheon, which contains the tombs of several Spanish kings and queens, is one of Europe's oldest fresco ceilings that dates from 1100. The frescoes in the Pantheon – many still vivid after eight centuries – are the reason this place is sometimes called Spain's Sistine Chapel.

This technique of painting frescoes – the art of using water-based pigments on walls freshly coated and still wet with lime plaster – has been practised since ancient times, and requires great skill on the part of the painter. When the plaster sets, the painting becomes an integral part of the wall. Some of the oldest and most beautiful examples of frescoes – from as far back as the 5th and 6th centuries – are found in Sigiriya in Sri Lanka and Ajanta in India.

The museum (through which one can enter the cloisters) has an extensive collection of handwritten books dating from the 12th century. These are ancient books that were not only written but also colourfully and laboriously illustrated by hand. I was especially taken up by one that had been painted in the 12th century showing David killing Goliath. One of the most famous possessions of this library is the beautifully preserved *Codex Biblicus Legionensis* – a generously illustrated Visigothic-Mozarabic Bible written in the year 960 AD. This was certainly a morning that provided a feast for the brain and the eyes.

We returned to the hotel by noon and checked out, walking to the Plaza Regal to rendezvous with Fadi and say farewell. He was taking the train from Leon to Sarria from where he was going to walk the last 100 km to Santiago as he had to get back to work by the end of the week. It seemed like ages since that day in the Pyrenees when Helle had stopped him in his downward track by shouting, "Hey, you are going the wrong way!" All of us had come a long way since that fortuitous meeting.

Leaving Fadi we met Roland with Praline and walked with them through the suburbs of Leon, passing the Plaza San Marcos with its *Parador* – originally a monastery dedicated to St Mark and now a magnificent hotel for tourists (and I suspect more affluent pilgrims). In front of the building is a lifelike statue of an exhausted pilgrim, seated on a bench and resting his weary legs while he gazes at the edifice of the monastery/*parador*.

We walked on, crossing the 16th century stone bridge over the river Bernesga and by 4 pm reached the municipal Albergue in Virgen del Camino – a very clean place with a comfortable living room having Wi-Fi and (in contrast to the unisex facilities in most of the municipal *albergues* in which we stayed) separate showers/toilets for men and women. The *albergue* was situated next to a place called *Casa Ejercitos* (House of Soldiers) which reminded me so much of a military establishment. My hunch was confirmed when I noticed two armoured cars and a Guardia Civil compound across the street – which I learned was the new regional headquarters of Regional Safety Group No. 6 of the Guardia Civil, which had been opened here by the Prime Minister just over a year previously in March 2010.

We showered and washed our clothes, and walked to the local bar where we had the pilgrim menu. Here we met Geoff Wilkinson from Canada and his Catalan father-in-law Enrico (Ric). The latter spoke Castilian Spanish, Catalan and English – and so was able to help us by translating and explaining the menu. Ric had been born in Spain but migrated to Canada as a young man and was walking the Camino for the sixth time. This walk however was special because he was bringing his 'Anglo-Canadian' son-in-law with him for the first time. Shivantha and I shared with them a very pleasant meal and two bottles of delightful Rioja wine which Ric selected from the restaurant's wine list

Tomorrow will mark four weeks to the day since we set off from St Jean Pied de Port.

Monday 16th May 2011: Virgen del Camino to Hospital de Orbigo

We left the *albergue* at 7.45 am and together with Roland and his donkey walked on empty stomachs for over 6 km until we reached a small place called San Miguel. Here we found a bar where we sat outside and had coffee and croissants, served by a patient lady. Unfortunately, when I went back inside and asked the man behind the bar, who appeared to be her husband, for water to fill my bottle, he refused.

When I went back outside and told Shivantha of this incident he was furious – and sprang to his feet to storm inside and give the owner a piece of his mind. I however prevailed on him to desist and let it ride. Reluctantly he complied with my request.

We strapped on our packs and walked on, each of us silent with his own thoughts.

Was I being prudent – or timid? Should I have let Shivantha go and tell the man off, not because it would have given us water but because, even with Shivantha's limited Spanish, his tone and body language would get the message across to the man that this was no way to treat visitors? At least the next pilgrim who came there would be treated with more respect. Maybe I had been too faint-hearted in challenging this rude and offensive man.

I discovered afterwards that while I was cogitating thus, Shivantha on the other hand was reflecting that maybe he had been too impetuous and that I was right – picking a fight on the other man's home turf, especially when we were not fluent in the language and had no support, was not wise. He had been reflecting on whether he was being righteously assertive – or just plain hot-headed?

As in most situations in life, perhaps the truth was somewhere in between.

Anyway, there were two good Camino Lessons here for both of us:

Camino Lesson Number Seven. ***When you are faced with a situation where someone – a shop or restaurant owner, a government official, even your boss at work – treats you disrespectfully, do not be afraid to be assertive and stand up for your right to be treated with respect. It may not change the immediate situation – but the person to whom you stand up will get the message and think twice before treating with disrespect the next disadvantaged person (the next black man, the next woman, the next foreigner) that they meet.***

And when you have to assert yourself and stand up to someone, do it with dignity – in a calm, calculated, even cold-blooded manner. Do not rush in hot-headed and give way to your temper!

Camino Lesson Number Eight: ***Truth depends on Perspective.***

You and I may witness the same scene – but how we interpret it, what conclusions we draw and how we react to it depends on our own particular perspective, which is influenced by a variety of factors such as upbringing, education and past experience.

We caught up with Roland and started talking about the incident – whereupon he told us that the man had even refused to let him leave Praline on the road outside the bar while he came inside for a cup of coffee. This was enough for Roland. He promptly decided not to give the man the privilege of his custom – and he moved on.

Interesting – an incident that certainly gave us something to reflect upon and taught us a couple of useful lessons.

Shivantha continued walking and talking (in French) with Roland, while I had the company of Bepe from Torino. We made it to Hospital de Orbigo, passing Villadangos del Páramo, San Martin del Camino and *Canal del Páramo* (the Canal of the Lover) at Presa de Cerrajera. There is a romantic story behind the building of this canal in the 11th century.

At this time, after the death of Almanzor and the fall of the Caliphate of Cordoba, many Mozarabic families (the Mozarabs were Arab converts to Christianity as well as Christians who had lived for generations in the Moslem-ruled parts of Spain, not changing their religion but educated in Arabic schools and adopting Arab dress, diet and culture with Arabic as their main language) had migrated north to the Kingdom of Leon and settled in the valley of the Orbiga river.

In Villaviciosa de la Ribeira lived a young man called Aliatar, son of the local governor. The family was originally from Seville. One day, while out riding he came to the village of Villazan, about 50 km south of his home – and there saw for the first time Zaida, the beautiful daughter of the local governor, herself a Granada-born migrant. Captivated by her beauty, he came back several times just to see her – and finally acquired the courage to meet her father, declare his love and ask for her hand in marriage.

Zaida's father was unsure of this suitor from a village far away and so decided to test him. After all, as they say in Sri Lanka, the father did not know "who's who" he was, even though the young man like himself was a Mozarab from an Andalucian family. He imposed a tough pre-condition – that Aliatar divert the water of the River Orbiga to reach his village. "The day the water of the River Orbiga passes in front of my door," he is reputed to have said, "I shall give you permission to marry my daughter."

Now this was a tough ask, because the river was about 2 km from Villazan, which in any case was situated at a higher level than the river. Undeterred by the condition imposed by his intended father-in-law, Aliatar enlisted the help of the locals, and aided by the skilled Mozarabic craftsmen in his village, achieved the impossible.

Once the waters flowed past Zaida's front door, the Villazan chief gave his consent, the lovers were married amid grand celebrations – and the arid land around Villazan was soon converted into lush fields.

Taken at one level, the tale illustrates what the power of true love can achieve and would make a great story for a movie or even a romantic novel like the Mills & Boon paperbacks my aunts used to read – but at another level, it reminds us of the fact that the lands of the Iberian peninsula benefited tremendously from the modern technology introduced during the seven centuries they were under Arab rule. Two Egyptian agronomists who came to southern Iberia in the 10th century – Ibn al-Bassal and Ibn al-Awaam – wrote manuals in which they adapted their expertise to local conditions. These books covered the design, construction and operation of water-wheels, pumps and irrigation channels, soil conservation and land management, plant propagation and animal husbandry. Working replicas of these innovative water wheels that scoop up water and convey it into irrigation channels can be seen in parts of Spain and Portugal even today – a fine example still waters the riverside gardens in the Portuguese city of Tomar.

The Arabs introduced plant varieties and foods from North Africa into Europe – and part of Spain's surviving Arab heritage are the old Arabic words that still exist in the Spanish language for many foods, for the irrigation systems that watered them and the warehouses in which food is stored.

These days, when the word 'Islamic' is used so frequently as a prefix to 'terrorism' and 'fundamentalism', there is a need for the world to be aware of the Islamic contribution to European civilisation that took root and then spread from southern Spain to the more northern parts of Europe. It would be true to assert that while the Dark Ages prevailed further north in Europe, the Arabs succeeded in making Iberia part of one of the world's most advanced civilisations.

At Hospital de Orbigo we checked into the parish hostel Albergue Parroquial which is maintained by a German confraternity. This antiquated building is actually the original parish hostel, surrounding a pretty cobblestoned central courtyard and pleasant garden. For lunch Shivantha and I went to the nearby Ristorante Los Angeles to have the pilgrim menu (fish soup, trout, fruit salad and a nice glass of white wine – all for €9) after which we came back to shower, wash clothes and rest.

In the evening Roland, whose culinary skills were honed as a chef at the restaurant in the Eiffel Tower, cooked us a fabulous meal – fish and prawns in a garlic and tomato sauce accompanied by salad and rice. We had two bottles of wine to complement the food and followed it with fruit salad and cheese. The three of us, together with Guy (also from France) and Anya from Belgium, sat at one of the trestle tables in the *albergue* garden and had a lovely evening. It was still light when we finished at nine – and as we started to clear up Anya observed, "I don't like finishing nice days!"

It is evenings like this – dinner in the open air at the Albergue Parroquial in Hospital del Orbigo – that we will retain as enduring memories of the Camino.

Tuesday 17th May 2011: Hospital de Orbigo to Astorga

In reaching Hospital de Orbigo we had completed 28 days and 500 km along our journey – and had reached the stage when we could without difficulty take a day's walk of 25 km in our stride.

We left the Albergue by 8 am after having had a bite for breakfast, and walked through Villares de Orbigo, where we stopped at a place called Bar Piris for coffee mainly because we spotted the sign outside the bar and the name 'Piris' reminded Shivantha of his friend Dimitri Peries with whom he went through University in Melbourne. While having our coffee he sent Dimitri a text message to let him know that we were having coffee with his namesake!

From there we reached Santibanez de Valdeiglesia – and then our way took us through some glorious natural woodland scenery, even passing a small isolated lake, before climbing to the Cruceiro of Santo Toribio. The stone cross here commemorates the 5th century Bishop Toribio of Astorga (446 to 460 AD) who on being banished from the city fell to his knees at this spot in an emotional final farewell to his diocese.

We had a lovely view from this place – down over the valley to Astorga and its twin-towered cathedral with the Montes de Leon visible beyond the city, the Pena Ubina and snowcapped peaks of the Cantabrian mountains to the north, and to the southwest the Sierra del Teleno whose highest spot is the Mountain named El Teleno which during Roman times was considered sacred to the god Mars. We stopped to have a snack here and make conversation with a young married couple – he American and she Italian – who were cycling to Santiago. Shivantha felt quite at home, speaking with them in Italian and English – and was pleased to discover that the couple had met when the man had gone to Italy as an exchange student and they found each other in the same class in university, just as he and Irma had done.

We reached Astorga in the early afternoon and checked into the Albergue Siervas de Maria, the new municipal hostel. After the usual shower and washing of clothes, we had a short rest and decided to venture to the Ristorante La Peseta for a good Maragateria meal.

A visit to Astorga, we had been told, would not be complete without sampling some Maragato food. The origins of these folk, the Maragatos, are lost – some believe that they are the descendants of North African tribes that came here during the Moorish invasions in the 8th century; others believe that they were actually a Visigothic group who, under their ruler King Mauregato, took refuge in the hills here and became isolated during the Moorish invasions. Whatever their origins, the hilly region surrounding Astorga is considered their traditional homeland, and it is here that they have been trying to maintain their ancient culture.

From those early times, the Maragatos were known as the muleteers of Spain. In those days, the country did not have many good roads along which wheeled vehicles could be used – so the transport of most goods had to be done using herds of mules that could reach parts of the land which carts and carriages could not. The Maragatos with their mules fulfilled this role of transport agents, developing a reputation as tough and trustworthy folk. It used to be said that entrusting one's cargo to a Maragato was a safe guarantee that it would be delivered intact at its destination, the muleteers being so utterly reliable for their honesty and fidelity.

The transport of fish from the coastal towns like A Coruña to Madrid was the monopoly of the Maragatos, who were entrusted even by the Royal family with this task. They used a relay system (similar to that used by the tiffin carriers of Colombo and Mumbai) which would get the fish to Madrid in four days; wells were built along the way and filled with snow during winter so that this would last for most of the summer as well. It was in these 'refrigerating chambers' that the fish was stored so it was kept fresh during the trip.

With the arrival of the railroad in the 19th century the requirement for muleteers decreased and the Maragatos lost their traditional livelihood. In the 40 or so villages around Astorga known as the Maragateria however, they have tried to maintain their traditional crafts, culture and cuisine. If we really wanted to indulge while here, we learned, we could order the *Cocido Maragato* – the traditional banquet with different meats (beef, chorizo, ham, pork, lamb, bacon, chicken, etc), cabbage, chickpeas, thick soups and desserts, with the dessert eaten first. However, we were warned, this would probably be the only meal our stomachs would be able to hold for the rest of the day. We decided to settle for a three-course meal – octopus for me and lamb for Shivantha – with a good bottle of Marqués de Cácares wine, at the end of which we were well satisfied.

As a town in which to spend a day of relaxation, Astorga was ideal. Once an important garrison town during the Roman occupation of Spain, it is today an attractive city with a fascinating array of historic buildings tightly packed within its medieval walls.

This was originally a Celtic settlement in the region known as Astorica; the Roman city of Astorica Augusta was founded around 14 BC. It was fortified with the arrival of the Xth Gemina Legion, and soon this garrison town grew in importance, being at the crossroads of many important military, trade and pilgrim routes, to become the capital of the Roman province of Asturia. We saw evidence of this early period in the Roman Museum in Plaza San Bartolome (next to the restaurant where we had our meal) where jewellery, gravestones, games and surgical instruments from the Roman period were tastefully displayed. We also watched an imaginative 15-minute video that depicted life during Roman times as seen through the eyes of a Greek slave Lyda. Close to the museum are the ruins of a Roman villa with parts of its mosaic floor still intact.

From the nearby lovely public gardens (*Jardin de Sinagogia* – the name indicating that once upon a time Astorga would have had a thriving Jewish community) we had a splendid view over the mountains that separate this region of Leon from Galicia in the west.

Astorga was a major centre for the production of chocolate ever since Spaniards brought back the secret of chocolate from South America in the 16th century. There is even *El Museo del Chocolate* here - a chocolate museum which allows visitors free tastings.

Astorga's twin-towered cathedral is ancient, being mentioned as early as the 3rd century. Today, it is a pleasing blend of Romanesque, Gothic and Renaissance architecture – and has an interesting cathedral museum displaying sculptures, jewellery, tapestries and paintings from ancient times. Just near the cathedral is an unusual grey granite building – the Palace of Gaudi. It was built at the site of the original Bishop's Palace that was destroyed by fire. In 1887 the bishop commissioned the famous architect Antonio Gaudi to rebuild it. Gaudi in his typical style commenced a masterpiece that would befit a Walt Disney movie, with neo-Gothic turrets, etc. But it would be only in 1961, several architects later, that the palace would finally be completed. Today it houses an eclectic collection – a beautiful little chapel with stained glass windows, a museum of the Camino de Santiago, and on the third floor a permanent exhibition of contemporary Leonese artists.

Of Astorga's modern buildings, the most intriguing for us was the town hall, the Ayuntiamento. Surmounting the Baroque façade of this building is an unusual clock, consisting of a large clock face, above which is a bell on either side of which are two figures – a man and a woman dressed in traditional Maragato costume. Each of the figures carries a hammer. Every hour, just before the clock should strike, the mechanical figures rotate – and strike the bell with their hammers.

We very much enjoyed our stay in Astorga. The only touristy thing we did *not* do was sample some of the traditional sweet delicacies – such as *Natillas* (vanilla pudding), *Mancenada* (sweet pastries) and the cake called *Maragato Roscon.*

Wednesday 18th May 2011: Astorga to El Ganso

We left the *albergue* around 8 am, walked through the Jardin de Sinagogia and along the ramparts of the old Roman wall to the cathedral and the Gaudi Palace to do our sightseeing. Going to the local post office to get stamps for my postcards and to recharge my phone, I saw a man in Spanish army uniform. He had three stars denoting his rank just beneath the name badge on his uniform, so assuming him to be a Captain like myself, I introduced myself as an officer in the Australian army, told him I was walking the Camino and asked if I could have a photo with him. He kindly obliged – his wife who was with him took the photo of us – and I discovered that he was Colonel Jose Millan Martin, the commanding officer of the artillery regiment stationed in Astorga. I also discovered that in the Spanish army while three small six pointed stars indicate the rank of *Capitán* (Captain) as in Australia and Sri Lanka, three large eight pointed stars represent a much higher rank: *Coronel* (Colonel)!

While I went to the post office, Shivantha was visiting a small shop in the Plaza Mayor, *La Cueva Merlin* (Merlin's Cave) where he bought a charm for himself and Irma. We sat down to have a coffee and some *patatas bravas* (fried potatoes) in the Plaza, at a table from which we had a good view of the famous Maragato clock over the town hall. We waited patiently for it to strike one o'clock, and having seen the performance of the costumed dolls striking the hour, we set off on our journey out of Astorga.

As we were walking today we came to realise that the scenery was starting to change – no more flat land with endless wheat fields on either side of the track. We have now reached a part of the Camino that is more like the Navarra region that we traversed soon after crossing over the Pyrenees. Ahead of us we could see the Montes de Leon, the highest part of our journey, which we would be tackling over the next few days.

We kept on, walking and talking and taking pleasure in the scenery around us until we reached Murias de Rechivaldo where we stopped for an Aquarius at Meson Eillar. Here we had an interesting conversation with the proprietor, a Spanish lady who could speak five languages. She told us that she had worked in France, England and Argentina – and had travelled to Myanmar, Thailand, Cambodia and other Buddhist countries. While we were chatting with her a German pilgrim arrived in a taxi to collect the jacket he'd absent-mindedly left behind earlier in the day – and we availed ourselves of the opportunity of a ride back with him to Santa Catalina (4 km ahead of us) from where we walked to El Ganso, one of the crumbing Maragato villages along the way. We checked into the Albergue Gabino and had our own food – tinned lentils, olives, bread and coffee. The evening was becoming chilly, so with the Dutch couple with whom we were sharing the room we managed to light a fire in the stove heater. The *hospitalero* later brought in some coal, and by bedtime the room was as warm as toast.

Thursday 19th May 2011: El Ganso to Rabanal del Camino

Although small and spartan, the rural Albergue Gabino had Wi-Fi, so after breakfast we managed to talk to Chitra and Irma on

Skype. We left around half past nine for the 7 km walk to Rabanal del Camino, a small village situated at the foot of Monte Irago. We had heard of the Albergue Gaucelmo at No. 4, Calle Calvario in this village which is run by the London-based confraternity of St James – and had decided that we would stay at this place.

Having arrived before opening time we spoke to the *hospitalero* there, Martyn Singleton, and walked over to the Posada Gaspar where we had a drink and then the pilgrim menu, which turned out to be a particularly good meal: seafood soup, *bacalao* (cod) and *arroz con leche* (a dessert of rice with milk) for me, and *Ensalada mixta* (mixed salad), Maragato veal and mousse for Shivantha. As usual we ordered a bottle of wine – Pensacal rosada – which turned out be quite a pleasant drop.

We returned to the *albergue* at 2 pm to check in. I have developed the convenient habit of washing my clothes while I shower – so with that duty done and my clothes hung out to dry, I spent a pleasant hour chatting with Martyn about his experience and his involvement with the Camino. He and his wife Pat, together with another English lady Jenny Carr, are all volunteer *hospitaleros*; the confraternity arranges a roster and sends out a team of two or three (who all pay their own airfares) to spend a fortnight running the *albergue*.

At 4.30 sharp – the *hospitaleros* were typically English in their punctuality – we sat around one of the trestle tables in the *albergue* courtyard and had afternoon tea with shortbread and biscuits. It is relevant here to recall that this very English custom of having afternoon tea with cakes and biscuits was introduced to England from Portugal by the Portuguese princess Catarina of Bragança when she came to England to marry King Charles the Second. Interestingly, this arranged marriage with Catarina provided the English king with a dowry of 350,000 pounds and the Portuguese colonies of Tangier and Bombay.

While sipping a pleasant cup of tea (it was so good that I had no doubt whatsoever that it was Ceylon tea) I chatted with a Dutch physiotherapist and an Italian called Salvatore. The latter spoke English with a very French accent. We have been discovering along the Camino a host of other travellers who are quite unlike us in age, origin, and interests – but so much like us in so many ways. In fact I am constantly reminded of the fact that there is much more that unites us folk than divides us.

After tea we went to the local *tienda* (grocery shop) which only opens from 5 to 8 pm to get chorizo, cheese and bread for dinner – and then walked into the 12th century Romanesque *Iglesia de Santa Maria* opposite the *albergue* at 7 pm to attend service. The service was conducted by Benedictine monks from the monastery of San Salvador del Monte Irago that is situated next door to the *albergue* and we had the pleasure of listening to some melodious Gregorian chanting by the two monks.

Sitting down in the *albergue* dining room to our frugal dinner of chorizo, cheese and bread, we were invited by Salvatore and his group of Italians at the table next to ours to share some of the pasta that they had cooked. As we sat together and enjoyed the meal and their company, we reflected that this is what would have taken place along the Camino since ancient times: the evening mealtime when pilgrims trekking to Santiago from various parts of the world sat together to share their food and their stories.

And along our own journey on the Camino, my son and I had experienced not just the kindness and generosity of fellow pilgrims but also the kindness of many ordinary folk along the way.

Friday 20th May 2011: Rabanal del Camino to Acebo

The previous night after dinner I sat in the *albergue* library in front of a log fire and wrote my journal. I have been maintaining this journal from the day I started the Camino – so that with the photographs I have been taking along the way, I hope in the years to come I will have something to reinforce the memories I will have of this special journey.

We left Rabanal around 8 am and made our way slowly uphill – the path ascends the Monte Irago through the villages of Foncebadon and Manjarin, passing *El Cruz de Ferro* (The Iron Cross) which marks the highest point of our journey. This cross, at the base of which pilgrims over the years have traditionally left a pebble or some token which they had brought from their homelands, rose up out of an immense cairn. I had planned to leave two pebbles here that I had carried with me from St Jean Pied de Port for this very purpose – one in memory of my mother and one on behalf of my friend Chris Brown in memory of his father Godwin -- but for some reason, I suddenly decided against it.

I had read that this Cruz de Ferro was where pilgrims on the journey to Santiago added their '*stone or other token of love and blessing to the great pile at the foot of the cross that witnesses our collective journeying*'. However, when I came upon the pile of stones, ribbons, cards, dried flowers, crumpled papers with messages written on them and sundry stuff piled high at the foot of the cross, all I saw was a heap of rubbish – not the sort of resting place that I envisaged for the token I had been carrying on this journey to remind me of my own mother. I told myself that my special pebble deserved a resting place more worthy of her, as did the pebble I was carrying for Chris. I was not sure where it would be – but I knew that when I came upon the place it would announce itself to me.

This journey has given me the opportunity to reflect on – and be grateful for – my mother who passed away fifteen years ago. Unlike my brother and sister, I was closer to my father than to her, and probably did not appreciate her as much in life as I should have. She was very fond of Shivantha her eldest grandson – as he was of her – because it was she who kept him and looked after him in his younger days when my wife and I were overseas. Over the past days he and I often talked of her, recalling various little incidents and sharing our memories.

I must confess that I have no idea what happens to us when we die. I believe however that we live on in the memories of others – and along the Camino I am sure that my mother was constantly with us.

The higher we climbed up the Monte Irago, the more spectacular the views became. Every once in a while we would stop just to enjoy the majestic mountain panoramas stretching out on our left. Along the way we met an Australian couple from Melbourne – and I discovered that Verna works as a venepuncturist at the medical clinic in my own suburb of Balwyn, situated just across the road from the supermarket where we do our regular shopping.

For our lunch break Shivantha suggested a quiet spot on the hillside with a beautiful view of the mountains spread out in front of us. We could see a herd of cattle on the mountain slope and hear the tinkling of their cowbells. We shared the food we had carried with us from Rabanal – a tin of beans, cheese, chorizo, yoghurt, a half-baguette of bread and an apple.

We made it shortly after 2 pm to Acebo – a quaint village consisting of a single narrow street lined on either side by old houses with low-slung balconies that almost touched our heads as we walked under them. For generations, Acebo has been sitting here on the side of the mountain about a thousand metres above sea level, looking out over the Celtic landscape. Both of us, father and son, felt something special about this place. The beautiful views of the surrounding mountains, the neat and well maintained houses with balconies overhanging the road, the ancient church, the friendliness not only of the people but also of the dogs and birds here (indicating a lack of fear) – we could not put a finger on precisely why it was so, but both of us got the feeling that El Acebo was welcoming us.

We decided to take a room for €35 at La Casa del Peregrino – and after the usual routine of washing ourselves and our clothes we sauntered down to the Casa restaurant to use their computer and internet connection to check emails and contact home. We sat at one of the tables with a bottle of De Muller Solimar Tinto Criaza 2008 red wine between us – the level in the bottle gradually diminishing as we read and wrote – until it was time for dinner to be served at seven. After dinner (the usual pilgrim menu!) we did a stroll through the village before retiring, taking time to look inside their quaint little 16th century village church of San Miguel situated at the far end of the village.

Saturday 21st May 2011: Acebo to Ponferrada

Saturday morning dawned, misty in these mountains, and we decided to take things easy, walking back to the Casa restaurant for breakfast. After having coffee, *bocadillos* and a *pastissette tortosa* (a Catalan pastry somewhat like a Sri Lankan 'patty' filled with a sweet pumpkin paste) we set off around ten on the next stage of our journey.

The path wended its way through beautiful woodland and groves of chestnut trees, where we could hear the sound of birds and even stop to admire the flowers. During the walk we came upon Riego de Ambros, another pretty mountain village with the typical balconies overhanging the street – and then the attractive medieval stone bridge that took us across the Rio Meruelo into another attractive village, Molinaseca, where we stopped for a beer and some empanadas.

It was getting quite hot in the middle of the day but we doggedly kept on to reach, by half past two, the town of Ponferrada (*Pons Ferrata* – named for the original bridge of iron that was built on the orders of bishop Osmundo of Astorga way back during the 11th century). Checking into the El Castillo hotel which I had booked on the internet while we were in Acebo we were allocated Room 205. We rested in bed for a couple of hours as we were both quite tired. Having recovered by about five we decided to visit the magnificent Templar castle.

The Camino is cluttered with churches, and along the Camino we have seen quite a few built in the typical octagonal architectural style – Eunate, Torres del Rio, Fromista – that are associated with the Knights Templar. The magnificent Castle at Ponferrada, originally a Roman citadel, is also a relic of these Knights. At the beginning of the 12th century it was taken over by them and refurbished as a fortified palace to give them a base from which they provided protection for pilgrims *en route* to Santiago de Compostela. Ponferrada in fact is the last major city on the French Way before Santiago.

To enter the impressive castle we had to go over a drawbridge crossing a moat. Its 12 original towers were said to have represented the 12 constellations, and its crenellated walls, narrow stone staircases and strangely shaped turrets certainly give it an air of medieval mystery.

That evening we had dinner with Verna and Ron, the couple from Melbourne we met the previous day. Interestingly, as a sequel to our meeting with Verna on the Camino, I dropped in to see her at her clinic in Balwyn the month after we returned – and in the course of conversation with the senior doctor at the practice, who had been a colleague of my wife at another clinic some years ago, I was offered a part-time job at this clinic which is just ten minutes' walk from our home. Now, I do a Saturday morning shift at this clinic every month – and it has all come about as a result of a chance meeting on the Camino!

Chapter 10: Death on the Camino

Sunday 22nd May 2011: Ponferrada – A Day of Rest

I was feeling quite tired when I woke up this morning, so having discussed the matter with Shivantha we decided to spend a day of rest (*una dia de descansar*) in Ponferrada. It may have been fatigue and dehydration resulting from the long walk in the heat yesterday or possibly an incipient viral infection – but whatever it was due to, a day of rest was called for.

Camino Lesson Number Nine: ***When your body tells you to take a rest, don't keep pushing on. Listen – and obey!***

We had breakfast, booked an extra night's stay at the hotel – and came back up to our room and slept. I got up around noon and went down for a bite but had no appetite and could only manage a vegetable sandwich, so I drank plenty of fluids and came back up to our room to sleep again.

Shivantha checked his emails and was stunned to see an email from Geoff Wilkinson – we'd had dinner with him and his father-in-law Enrico Luis in Virgen del Camino a few days previously – to tell us that his father-in-law had passed away in his sleep the previous day at the *albergue* in Cacabelos. Although we had heard of pilgrims dying on the Camino, and even seen some of the memorials to them that had been erected along The Way, this was the first encounter we had with death taking away a fellow pilgrim – one with whom we'd shared a meal and a glass of wine less than a week ago.

In Geoff's email he mentioned that he had to come back to Ponferrada that weekend to attend to the formalities of getting Enrico's death certificate and to arrange for the cremation and transportation of the remains to Canada – and that he was going to be staying at the Hotel El Castillo – the selfsame hotel in which at that very minute we were reading his email to us.

We quickly went down to reception to find out whether Geoff was still in the hotel – and discovered him to be staying in Room 207, which was the very next one to our own.

We immediately called Room 207. Geoff was there and soon he was down at reception. He was being taken that afternoon by Jesus, the *hospitalero* at the Cacabelos Albergue where Enrico had died, for Sunday lunch with his family – but we arranged to meet after he returned to have dinner together.

Shivantha and I returned to our room, rested for a couple of hours and although still very tired, went out for a short stroll to the castle to get some sunlight and fresh air. In the evening we took Geoff to have dinner with us at one of the restaurants close to the hotel. Over our meal of gazpacho, calamari, *pimientos*, *revueltos* and wine, I explained to Geoff one of our Sri Lankan traditions. Whenever a death occurs in a home in Sri Lanka, it is our custom that no fire can be lit and no cooking can be done in that house until the funeral ceremony is over. As a result, it is customary for neighbours, relatives and friends to bring food for the bereaved family during this period of mourning – which is a way of ensuring that during the time of grieving they have a constant stream of visitors to provide them with support and sustenance. Nobody in Sri Lankan society is allowed to grieve alone.

In this way, we told Geoff that we were treating him as we would a family member back home – meaning that he would be our guest and that we would be paying for the meal, which would allow us to provide him with food and company in his time of bereavement. We spent a long time over the meal that evening, and when we finally got up to leave Geoff confessed that he was glad of the opportunity of being with supportive friends in the company of whom he was able to unburden himself at this very sad time.

We have discovered that folk on the Camino come from different countries and different backgrounds, they are of different ages and different religious persuasions – but they all have a common purpose: taking time out of the routine of their daily lives to pursue a common goal. And with *compañeros* like this you feel you can talk openly about matters that you would not normally discuss with your neighbours and colleagues.

Monday 23rd May 2011: Ponferrada to Villafranca del Bierzo

We took it easy this morning, strolling over to the nearby bar to have coffee, yoghurt and pastries for breakfast before leaving the hotel around 11.45 to walk to the Estacion de Autobus and take the bus to Villafranca del Bierzo. Half an hour, 25 km and €1.40 later we were in Villafranca – one of many similarly named Villafrancas, towns populated by pilgrims from France who had decided after making the pilgrimage to settle down here and not return home.

We walked to the Hotel Burbia on the far side of the Rio Burbia and got a room on the second floor with a lovely view over the river. I spoke to the hotel owner in Spanish (his English was as limited as was my Spanish) but with his ten-year-old daughter Claudia I started a conversation in English because I was told that she studies English in school. She told me that she was off school today with a "sore throat" – but broke into giggles when with mock disbelief I told her (in both English and Spanish) that I was a doctor and that she did not look ill enough to be missing school!

After the usual shower and washing of clothes, we watched the movie *Forrest Gump* which Shivantha had on his computer, and then strolled into town to have a look at the sights. Villafranca is a pretty town with several historic buildings – the most significant being the 12th century *Iglesia de Santiago*, the beautiful Romanesque church dedicated to Santiago with the *Puerta del Perdon* (Door of Forgiveness) as its northern entrance. In ancient times, one of the Spanish popes decreed that pilgrims who had made it this far but were unable to complete the journey to Santiago due to ill health or infirmity (the path from here through the mountains of Galicia gets more difficult) could obtain at this church the same indulgence that they would receive at the altar of the cathedral in Santiago.

Having seen the Collegiata Church and sat a while in the municipal garden, we stopped at a little bar overlooking the gardens to have coffee, bought some food from the nearby food shop and then sat by the river outside our hotel enjoying a pleasant meal of tinned *zamburinos* (small scallops), olives, asparagus, bread and wine. I borrowed two plates and glasses from the hotel – causing a bit of consternation at first when I asked for two "*plantas*" (irons) instead of "*platos*" (plates)!

Tuesday 24th May 2011: Villafranca del Bierzo to Ruitelan

We left Hotel Burbia by 8 am and stopped at the bar near the municipal garden where we had a drink the day before, to have a coffee and chocolate *napolitana* – and then walked along the Pradela route through a steep incline that skirted a pine forest, chestnut woods and some smallholdings with great views back to Villafranca over the Valcarce valley and mountains.

This Pradela route was more taxing than the alternative route following the N VI road because it climbed steeply to 930 metres before coming down to Trabadelo. However, we took this path as we felt it would be closer to Nature – and we were not disappointed. We were surrounded by a panoramic view of gigantic green hills with the distant mountains on the horizon enveloped in a blue haze.

We walked along enjoying the moment – listening to the sounds of birds and crickets, watching bees and butterflies and having glorious views to Villafranca behind us and the Dragonte mountains to our left.

Later on we passed pylons carrying high tension wires (we could even hear the crackle of electricity passing along the wires!) and also the massive concrete supports for the A6 Autopista. When a heavy truck drove along the motorway, the sound created was like distant thunder.

We reached Portela da Valcarce, about 15 km along our journey, around noon and stopped at the hotel there for refreshment. My shirt was soaked through and I took the opportunity of changing into a dry one from my pack – and hanging the wet shirt out to dry from my backpack. We needed two Aquarius drinks each and then had the substantial menu of the day – which forced us to rest till around 3 pm before resuming our walk. From Portela da Valcarce (the name comes from *Vallis Carcare* meaning 'gateway to the narrow valley') to Ambasmestas (the name is a combination of 'waters' *Aguas* and 'mix' *Mestas,* since this is where the Rio Balboa joins the Rio Valcarce) Shivantha carried my backpack as well as his until I got my walking legs working again.

We continued, the Rio Pereje always on our left, until we reached Ruitelan. Walking by the river along this stretch was very pleasant – picturesque stone houses, quaint wooden bridges, small slate walls and the constant sound of gurgling waters. In due course we found the Pequeno Potala *albergue* run by Luis and Miguel, a quaint place which has a lot of Tibetan influence in its pictures, decorations and the gentle music and

Buddhist chants that waft through the rooms. We were too full after our big lunch at Portela de Valcarce to avail ourselves of the shared meal provided here – so we sat out in the courtyard in the evening enjoying the view over the green mountains. I wrote my journal while Shivantha spent this time strumming a guitar he found there.

We then spent a pleasant hour chatting with some of the other pilgrims staying there – a young student from Denmark and a lady from France. The Danish lad told us he would return home after the Camino to commence university studies, while the French lady had just retired after spending all her working life as a secondary school teacher. So many times along The Way have we made this discovery: we are all so different – in our origins, our professions, in the stages of our lives at which we find ourselves undertaking the Camino, in the motivation that each of us has to walk the Camino – but we are all united in having this extraordinary quest for something that is different to our ordinary lives. We are in effect drawn together by a conviviality that arises from the sharing of hardships so far away from home.

Tomorrow we will set off on the last leg of our journey, starting with a steep climb to enter the land of the Celtic peoples – the autonomous region of Galicia in the northwestern corner of Spain.

Wednesday 25th May 2011: Ruitelan to O Cebreiro

We were woken at 6 am by gentle Tibetan music in our rooms, and after breakfast (for the first time on our journey we were offered muesli, but I was the only one to serve myself some) we left the Pequeno Potala to tackle the steep climb to O Cebreiro which is 1310 metres above sea level. I took it slowly and was able to enjoy some amazing views over the mountains and valleys. In some places we could hear cowbells in the distance even though we could not see the cows themselves. When it was midday we sat on the mountain side and had our baguettes with cheese and chorizo.

We stopped at Laguna to drink some Aquarius (I was so thirsty that I drank a whole litre) and here we saw our first *Horreo* or *palloza* – conical-roofed circular or oval structures made of rough stone that had straw-thatched roofs. We were told that in ancient days these structures were dwelling places where whole families lived with their livestock; they had sloping floors which allowed the family to sleep at a higher level while the cattle were confined to the lower portion. This ensured that the animals' droppings did not contaminate the humans' sleeping quarters. Today these *pallozas* are used to store grain, very similar to the *veebissas* of Sri Lanka in which rice is stored after the harvest.

In due course we crossed over from the province of Leon to the autonomous region of Galicia and reached O Cebreiro around 2 pm.

This ancient Celtic village is like something out of one of those much-loved children's comic books by Goscinny and Uderzo about Asterix the Gaul. In fact, with its moisture-laden air and swirling mists, the conical straw-thatched houses of grey stone and surrounding green hills, it could have been the same village from which Asterix and Obelisk came. We had reserved a room at the San Giraldo de Aurillac Hostal which is owned by a niece of Don Elias Valina de Sampayo, the parish priest who did so much in his lifetime to restore the popularity of Camino. It was he who had the idea of marking the route with the yellow arrows which we pilgrims have found so useful. His tomb and bespectacled bust in the grounds of the church, *La Iglesia de Santa Maria Real* (Royal Church of Saint Mary) that dates from the 9th century, testify to the respect in which he is held in these parts.

The church is associated with a miracle that is said to have taken place in the 12th century. The story goes that on a

Plate 13

13A: Santiago Peregrino – St James the Pilgrim

13B: Santiago Matamoros – St James the Moorslayer

Plate 14

14A: Waymarker – Yellow arrow with a headless Santiago

14B: Waymarker –Scallopshell on pavement

Plate 15

15A: Along the Way in Galicia

15B: On the Way between Rabenal and Acebo

Plate 16

16A: Village in Navarra

16B: Country Road Take Me Home

particularly cold and stormy Sunday morning in winter the priest was preparing for the morning Mass but not a single resident had turned up, so he decided to dispense with the service and go back home to his warm meal. Unfortunately for him, just as he was about to step out and close the door of the church, there turned up a peasant from the valley who had struggled up the hill all alone, braving the icy winds, to attend the service and receive Holy Communion. The priest was reluctant to celebrate Mass for just this one man, and tried to dissuade him and send him away - but the man was adamant.

Reluctantly the priest began the service – and when he reached the part of the Mass where he held up the bread and wine to consecrate them as the body and blood of Jesus Christ, to the amazement of both priest and peasant, the bread turned into flesh and the wine into blood.

Whatever credence one might give to this story today, it served its purpose in the old days. Pilgrims walking to Santiago just *had* to visit the church and the village where this miracle occurred – which would naturally have ensured that the inns in O Cebreiro would have regular custom and the church would be the beneficiary of regular donations. Today the original chalice (cup) and patten (plate) which were used in the service at which the miracle took place are kept in a high-tech bulletproof glass vault within the church for visiting pilgrims to venerate.

In the early evening we explored the town and then had the pilgrim menu (garlic soup and trout, and for dessert the local speciality *queso y membrillo* (cheese and quince jam). While Shivantha went after dinner to have a drink (or drinks?) with Sarah, Patricia, Pablo and Carlos (pilgrims of his age group from various parts of Spain), I stayed chatting with Giuliano who hails from a small suburb of Bologna in which the Lamborghini plant is situated. He had retired on May 1st having worked 40 years for the Italian bank Unicredito, and had planned to complete the

Camino, take a holiday until the end of July and then decide what he will do with the rest of his life. We discussed how times have changed – just a hundred years ago, folk retired from full-time work at 55 or 60 and were dead by 65, while today most of us are forced to retire when we reach the age of 60 or 65 after which we then have 20 to 30 years of life left. How will 21st century men (and women, who have an average life span even longer than men do) utilise the 'grey years' of their lives in a way that is fulfilling for them and useful for society?

As I walked back to our accommodation, I reflected: how will I utilise the rest of my life? The advantage of being a general practitioner is that I could continuing working as long as health and memory last. My friend and colleague Frank is about ten years older than I am and still works full-time at our clinic – and a few years ago I met one of my father's classmates, Granville, still working three half-days a week as a GP at the age of 85. Being a doctor, established in a position to help patients and make a difference in their lives, I derive a lot of job satisfaction and self-esteem – and reasonable financial remuneration – from my work. I believe that of the many careers that one can choose, Medicine can provide you with one of the best combinations of happiness, recognition and regular income. But for how long will I want to work? How long will my body and brain let me continue working? Will I want to keep working, getting up and going to the clinic or the university every day for the rest of my life – or will I want to spend more and more time in leisure activities such as reading, writing, travelling and relaxing with the family?

I don't yet know the answer to these questions. But at least I am thinking about them.

Thursday 26th May: O Cebreiro to Triacastella

We woke to a cool and damp morning with the feel of moisture in the air. Having had coffee with Giuliano, we left at 8.45 for the downhill trek to Triacastella. Surrounded by vividly green hills shrouded in the morning mist we trudged along country roads whose sides were thick with green foliage sprouting from the rich black earth - and whose bitumen provided us with the sight and smell of fresh cow dung. The smell is often referred to as the 'scent of Galicia'.

We did have a few uphill inclines, including one to *Alto de Poro*, the highest spot on the Camino in Galicia. Arriving in Triacastella we found the Albergue Xacobeo (not *Jacobeo* as in Castilian Spanish but *Xacobeo* as in Galician, the language of this region) and checked in. Our main meal for the day was in the Xacobeo restaurant – *Caldo Gallego* (a thick hot vegetable soup), paella, Sonyal white wine and the Galician speciality *queso con mile* (cheese with honey). Shivantha took a photo of me enjoying this high-calorie high-fat dish to show the 'Diet Police' (my wife and daughter) back home. Of course I conveniently subscribe to the view that after one walks for five hours, whatever fats and sugars one eats get metabolised and are incapable of increasing one's levels of either blood glucose or cholesterol.

Giuliano came afterwards to have a glass of wine with us, and we were joined by Marcel Delorme from Quebec and Charlie Pereira and Alison McMahon from New York. She is a film-writer and knows a couple of Shivantha's teachers from AADA. We sat chatting with them until 9 pm before retiring to our room for the night.

Friday 27th May 2011: Triacastella to San Mamed del Camino

We left the Albergue Xacobeo by 7.30 am, stopping in their restaurant for a breakfast (*desayuno)* of freshly squeezed orange juice, *napolitana* and coffee, before walking along a pleasant path beside the Oribio river, its gentle sound of flowing water a constant companion as we made our way westwards.

Our journey today was along timeless woodland paths (called *correidoiras*) that were lined on either side by bluebells as well as shady birch and oak trees, with the gurgling sound of the river never far away - and ancient country roads that went past farms from which emanated the smell of freshly cut grass and freshly passed cow dung.

By half past eleven we reached the huge Benedictine monastery of San Samos, established in the 6th century and dedicated to San Julian. It is one of the oldest and largest in Europe. What was most impressive was the sheer size of this place. On our guided tour of the monastery we saw its collection of paintings and frescoes, both ancient and modern, as well as both of the monastery's cloisters. The first was over 50 metres long and one of the largest cloisters we have seen, while the second smaller cloister had in its centre a beautiful Baroque fountain. We noticed some intriguing pictures among the modern murals in this monastery – one depicting a beautiful nun with the unmistakeable face of Sophia Loren, and another that showed a group of cherubs – four obviously Caucasian (as most cherubs are) and one distinctly Afro-Carribean or perhaps even Sri Lankan in appearance. "*Tha*," whispered Shivantha with a mischievous smile as we stood in front of the mural to admire it, "did you see the Token Black?"

After our tour of the monastery we made a short detour to see the *Capilla del Salvador*, the tiny 9th century chapel built in the Mozarabic style. It is also called *La Capilla de Cipres* (The Cypress Chapel) because of the ancient cypress tree that stands in front of it.

Having seen this simple rustic church we walked the ten kilometres to San Mamed del Camino and checked in to the peaceful private *albergue* run by Paloma and Lena. We met their son Diego, and while chatting with him discovered that he had been to Sri Lanka with a charitable organisation called *Fundacion Cofares*. Since then the family has been supporting a child in Sri Lanka – a girl at Sri Sumangala Balika Vidyalaya in Matara.

We participated in the communal dinner – lentil soup, tortilla, salad, apple and *Tarta de Santiago* (an almond-rich pastry decorated with the Santiago cross). I paid €15 for a DOC bottle of Reserva Rioja wine which we shared with Tom Guillame, a young Belgian who was walking the Camino with his backpack and guitar. Borrowing a guitar from Diego, Shivantha and Tom jammed together – after which several of us had a singsong in the *albergue* garden. Even I (inspired, no doubt by the Reserva Rioja) composed a song for the occasion:

> ***"How many miles must a pilgrim walk on – before he can call it a day?***
>
> ***And how many meals must a pilgrim consume – before he detests pilgrim meals?***
>
> ***And how many drinks must a pilgrim knock down – before he can sing you a song?***
>
> ***The answer my friend, is blowing in the wind – the answer is blowing in the wind!"***

It was a very enjoyable evening.

Friday 28th May 2011: San Mamed del Camino to Portomarin

We left the Albergue early the next morning, around 7.30, and did a quick walk to Sarria, which is just over 100 km from Santiago. It is at the town of Sarria that all those who want to walk the minimum distance required to obtain a *Compostela* join the Camino – for it is accepted by the Catholic church that a pilgrim must walk at least a hundred kilometres to Santiago (it is 200 km if travelling on bicycle or horseback) to receive the blessings, the indulgences and the official *Compostela* certificate of completion.

We continued on a further 8 km to Barbadello, having to climb up a particularly steep slope, so Shivantha carried my pack together with his own.

We were walking thus, me without any backpack while Shivantha was having one pack in front of him on his chest and the other strapped to his back, when we passed a large German pilgrim heavy laden with a monstrous pack on his back that must have weighed about 20 kg. He looked with envy at me as I walked packless behind this young man carrying two packs, then stopped and observed, "You haf a very good friend."

I laughed and responded, "He is not my friend, he is my son." Whereupon the man replied, "Then your son is a very good friend for you."

And it is only when someone else makes an observation like this that you stop, reflect, and then realise: "That sums it up perfectly."

We stopped at Barbadello to rehydrate ourselves with the usual Aquarius plus a snack – *empanada atun* (tuna pastry) for Shivantha and *bocadillo con sardinas y tomate* (sandwich with sardine and tomato) for me – and carried on walking. We passed through many small hamlets. This is rural Galicia at her best: wet and green with the strong smell and soft squelch of liquid cow dung under foot.

We had further 'Aquarius breaks' at Morgrade and Mocadeiro. Soon after the latter we met up with a pilgrim from Baltimore, Annette Argall. She had studied Spanish at University, taught in Madrid for a while, had volunteered as a *hospitalera* and is now on the board of American Pilgrims on the Camino. Having just been to Salamanca to inspect an *albergue* which the American confraternity had provided assistance to upgrade, she was walking the Camino this time from Ponferrada to Santiago. I enjoyed chatting with her – and thus walking and talking, we did not notice the kilometres slipping by until we came to the bridge over the river Mino. Crossing over this bridge we walked up the steps on the far side into Portomarin – and checked into the Albergue Ferramenteiro.

Today's journey was probably the longest stretch we have done in one day – 27 km. Without realising it, I have become fitter and stronger as I walked along the Camino these past five weeks – and I am sure, despite all the pilgrim meals and good Spanish wine, I have also lost quite a few kilograms along the way.

Saturday 29th May 2011: Portomarin to Portos

Leaving the *albergue* early we made good time to Gonzar where we stopped for a drink and snack – and for me to change my sweat-soaked shirt.

Moving on from here we walked on briskly. But at a fork in the path where surprisingly there was no yellow arrow to guide us, we started heading along one of the tracks and had progressed some distance along it when we were hailed by a man on the other track, clapping and calling to attract our attention. When we stopped, he quickly came after us to bring us back to the correct path. As he came closer, Shivantha turned to me incredulously and said, "Is this who I think it is?" – and it turned out to be Jasek, the Polish pilgrim Shivantha had helped exactly a month previously in Uterga.

We might not have recognised Jasek if not for the unusual little wooden cross he wore around his neck. The man looked well and clean-shaven, and was walking back home having completed his pilgrimage to Santiago. How lucky we were to run into this Pole again to guide us onto the correct path! Now it was my turn to use one of the very few Polish phrases I knew and say, "*Dziekuje bardzo*" ("Thank you very much"). Although our Polish was as limited as his English, smiles, warm handshakes and hugs conveyed our happiness at meeting each other again – and the fortuitous way in which we were each there to help the other in a time of need.

We walked on – in the correct direction shown to us by Jasek – and reached the ten-bed Albergue La Calzada at Portos around 2.30. We stopped here to refresh ourselves – and while we were having our usual Aquarius and *bocadillos*, Alison and Charlie stopped by and joined us. When I told them of my interest in walking an extra 5 km off the Camino route to see the 14th century *Iglesia de San Salvador*, an ancient seat of the Knights of Santiago, Alison (who is also interested in this aspect of the history of the Camino) decided to accompany me .

Although a light drizzle had developed, we left Shivantha and Charlie chatting over a beer and walked an hour each way to the hamlet of Vilar de Donas to see the simple Romanesque granite church with its richly carved doorway, beautiful frescoes and poignant stone effigies. One fresco in particular caught my eye – a pair of elegant women of aristocratic appearance in fine garments. Were these the *'Donas'* from which the place got its name? What is the connection to the Knights of Santiago whose tombs are here in the church? So many questions – Alison and I had a lot to talk about as we made our way back. She is collecting material for a novel she is writing based on the Camino and set in 11th century Spain.

Charlie and Alison decided to go on to Palais de Rey but Shivantha and I decided to stay here. We were fortunate to be the only *peregrinos* in the place and enjoyed having it to ourselves. Most people stop here only for a drink and a bite before going on, it being just 5 km to the big town of Palais de Rey. We appreciated this *albergue* for its charming rural setting – a tranquil garden with a metal crucifix and a *horreo* (a wooden 'thing' on stilts constructed for drying and storing maize). The stilts, we were told, are topped with metal sheets to prevent rats climbing into the chamber where grain is stored.

After we bade goodbye to Alison and Charlie we showered, washed clothes, wrote our journals, relaxed over a bottle of DOC Casa Viejo Rioja wine and had a leisurely dinner of tortillas, salad and ice cream – with the proprietor providing us each a cup of coffee on the house

Today certainly was a fortuitous day. The highlight was meeting Jasek again and realising that the person you have the opportunity to help in one situation will often be there, perhaps when you least expect it, to repay your good deed somewhere and sometime else in the future. We had enjoyed spending time with Charlie and Alison and realising how much all of us had learned from each other.

Most enjoyable however was the opportunity of having a relaxing evening to ourselves in this peaceful location, sharing a bottle of wine and chatting with my son. After we finished the Camino, he would be going back to New York and I to Melbourne – and we did not know when we would see each other again. My father used to say that as parents all we can do is give our children a good education, provide them with good values – and try to be a good role model for them. After they grow up, we have no control over where they will spend the rest of their lives or what career they follow, for that is a choice they have to make for themselves.

After a pleasant walk, we had a pleasant talk. Like the walrus and the carpenter in Lewis Carroll's poem we talked of many things – although of course we didn't eat any oysters.

Monday 30th May 2011: Portos to Palas de Rey

After such a relaxing evening we took it easy in the morning, languidly having a breakfast of coffee, mushroom tortilla and *boccadillos* with chorizo before leaving the Albergue la Calzada around ten.

The walk to Palas de Rey was just over 5 km; the hotel we were planning to stay in was full, as were many of the hotels in town (it appears that this place does very well out of the pilgrim trade) but we managed to get a comfortable twin bed room for €30 at a small *pensione* a bit off the Camino. The name Palas de Rey means 'Palace of the King' – but there is little evidence of either palaces or kings in this town of shops, hotels and restaurants.

We showered and gave our clothes to the nearby *lavanderia*, after which I walked to the local post office to buy an 8GB memory stick so I could transfer all the writings I had saved on Shivantha's computer. While I was gone he phoned the US Embassy in London and arranged his visa interview for June 14th, reserved the Hotel Villa de Rice in Lisbon for both of us to stay in on June 7th, and booked his flight from Lisbon to London for June 10th. He had decided that after completing the Camino he would travel with me to Lisbon to see Chitra, because he had not seen his mother for over a year – but he planned to keep this a secret from her and surprise her when she arrived in Lisbon on June 8th.

We walked down to the restaurant on the ground floor of our *pensione* and had the pilgrim menu, after which I went back up and slept from 3 to 5 pm. Dinner was a light meal – *queso con higos* (cheese with figs) and a plate of assorted meats with a bottle of white wine – and we spent a long time chatting over the meal. Soon our adventure would be coming to an end. We have walked and Time has flown – and we are just three days away from our destination. We are certainly looking forward to reaching Santiago – but we have mixed feelings, saddened as we realise that our journey together will soon be ending.

Tuesday 31st May 2011: Palas de Rey to Ribadiso

We left our comfortable lodgings around 7 am and soon found a bar to have coffee and chocolate croissants for breakfast. We kept up a steady pace, stopping at Mato Casanova for a drink and a snack, and then walking on through Melide and Boente to reach the *albergue* at Ribadiso de Baixo by 2 pm. We had done about 5½ hours' walking and were very tired – but very content with our achievement. I conveyed my thoughts to Shivantha as we checked in: "I am fatigued – but I feel well."

This *albergue* has a lovely setting by the river, situated close to where a picturesque old bridge crosses the river Iso. It stands at the site of a 15th century pilgrim hospital built and maintained by Antonine monks. We had a room with two bunk beds and so had to share it with just two other men.

We sat for a while by the river, enjoying the spring sunshine, and then went to the bar next door for a late lunch/early dinner. *Lentilas*, mixed salad, *calamares*, and *pimientos de padron* (a dish of capsicums which was *very* good) with two bottles of a most acceptable Galician wine between us – this was a fitting reward for our long day of walking. Well satisfied by our repast and tired out after our efforts, we turned in early.

Wednesday 1st June 2011: Ribadiso to Santa Irene

June has arrived and we have completed six weeks on the Camino. We took our time leaving Ribadiso – stopping at the bar opposite the *albergue* to have a good breakfast of two glasses of orange juice, two croissants and two cups of coffee each before we left on our way at 9 o'clock. We followed the natural shaded pathways stopping at Calle for a drink and at O Emplame for a bite. About 20 km from Ribadiso we came upon the little hamlet of Santa Irene - and made a decision to stay here at the Albergue Santa Irene. It is a pretty, well maintained house which functions as a private *albergue*. The house itself belongs to the *Dona* of an old Galician family whose housekeeping staff run the place. It has room for just 15 people, with five double bunks downstairs and five beds upstairs.

We gave our pilgrim clothes to be laundered while Shivantha stitched the tear in his trousers (a recurring problem ever since we left St Jean Pied de Port). After showering we sat and relaxed until dinner time - initially in the lovely little rear garden and later, as it got dark, in the tastefully furnished living room. There were several coffee table books - in Spanish but with beautiful photographs - of Galicia, which we enjoyed looking through over a bowl of olives and a bottle of Ribeiro wine.

Dinner was a communal meal - hot soup, well prepared fish and tinned fruit - which we shared at our table with a Danish mother and daughter and two Spanish men.

Thursday 2nd June 2011: Santa Irene to Santiago de Compostela

This morning we set off (as usual, the last pilgrims to leave the *albergue*) on the last stage of our journey to Santiago de Compostela. Passing through woods of eucalyptus whose scent reminded us of Australia we stopped at Arca, where we met some Italian pilgrims from Milano and Napoli. Hearing them talking away in Italian, Shivantha greeted them, wished them "Buon Camino" in Spanish - and then proceeded to ask in Italian whether they were looking forward to reaching Santiago that day. They were quite surprised to hear this very non-Italian-looking man speaking to them in their own language, and soon he fell into conversation with them, pulling out his laptop to show them pictures of him and Irma in Firenze. We had coffee with them and many photographs were taken.

Walking through the woods we recognised the scent of gum trees – which have been cultivated here since 1865, when some over-enthusiastic entrepreneurs got the idea of introducing eucalyptus trees from Australia to provide cheap timber for the local construction industry. Nurtured by Galicia's abundant rainfall and rich soil, the gum trees thrived – and today are as much of an introduced pest in Spain as the rabbit and the cane toad are in Australia.

We were soon passing through Lavacolla, a place whose name had intrigued me from the time I first heard it. Apparently this was where the pilgrims, dusty and begrimed and with little opportunity to have a decent wash during their long walk to Santiago, stopped to cleanse themselves before they reached the cathedral. The most important aspect of this cleaning ritual was to wash their backsides – from which the place got its name: *lavar* (wash) + *culo* (backside). Today Lavacolla is the site of Santiago's airport – and the river at which the pilgrims used to perform their human ablutions is no longer evident, dried up no doubt by the growth of human habitations.

From Lavacolla it is about 5 km to Monte de Gozo, the Mountain of Joy from which pilgrims would get their first glimpse of the spires of Santiago. Unfortunately these days the view of the cathedral is obscured by trees, but there is a grand monument here commemorating the visit of Pope John Paul II to Santiago, which makes up for the lack of view. The hill itself is being reshaped to provide a vast sports complex for the city. We met Alison and Charlie here and went with them to the restaurant at the Monte de Gozo *albergue* where we had a nice meal – and continued on to reach the Albergue Acuario, a rather crowded 'New Age' type of place with bunks so close together that we felt packed in like sardines. Checking in and leaving our packs here we walked along the pilgrims' way-marked trail, aware that we still had about 3 km to reach our final destination, the cathedral of Santiago de Compostela.

We walked along narrow roads, our footsteps quickening as we approached the cathedral. We passed a young man standing under the arch, incongruously playing his Galician bagpipes - and then suddenly we were sauntering into the huge Plaza de Obradoiro.

Bordered by the town hall *Pazo de Raxoi* on its north, the *Parador Hostal dos Reis Catholicos* with its beautiful Renaissance façade on its east, the *Colegio de San Jeronimo* (part of the university) on its west and the cathedral on its south, the huge plaza is certainly an impressive place. We walked on to stand directly in front so we could look up at the imposing façade of the Cathedral - and then turned to each other, grinning from ear to ear. Eight hundred kilometres and 45 days since we had left St Jean Pied de Port - we had reached our destination.

It was then that Shivantha grabbed me in a bear hug and said, "*Thaththi*, I have never told you this before, but I love you very much."

I still do not know whether he had prepared those words or if they just came to him spontaneously. I struggled for a bit to respond with something equally profound but I had to give up, because there were tears in my eyes and I was overcome emotionally.

As I thought about it afterwards, I realised that during this journey, I had the awesome opportunity of getting to know my son as an adult. The little boy I used to carry on my shoulders many years ago, the mischievous child with the toothy grin and his mother's dimple who had to be reminded to do his homework, to fill up and send in his application forms on time, not to forget to do this or that important thing, was now a man, an adult who was able to accomplish things as well as (and sometimes, I had to admit, even better than) his father.

Having seen Shivantha on the Camino, I could (at the risk of quoting another Father who is recorded in the Bible as saying these very words a couple of thousand years ago) now say with confidence: "This is my beloved son, in whom I am well pleased." In fact, if he were not my son, I told myself, he is the sort of person who I would have selected as my friend.

And it had been worth making this arduous journey just to experience that moment - and to hear him say what he said to me in the Plaza of Santiago de Compostela.

Having finally reached Santiago we spent some time basking in the late afternoon sun in the Plaza de Obradoiro, greeting old friends like Giuliano from Italy, Marcel from Quebec and the many Italians we had met along the way. Walking with these others, despite our different backgrounds and our various reasons for undertaking the Camino, we had shared a common purpose which opened the door to comradeship and cooperation. Our walking together along this path encouraged a kind of solidarity - which has now been strengthened by our soul-strengthening achievement of completing the journey.

In St Jean Pied de Port I had picked up a white pebble that I had decided to carry along the Camino in memory of my mother. At the request of my friend Chris Brown, I had agreed to also carry a black pebble in memory of his father Gordon Brown who had been my patient for many years. A devout Catholic, Gordon used to constantly remind me that his survival after developing naso-pharyngeal cancer was due to "God having looked after me and Dr Sanjiva having made the diagnosis so early." My own view was that God had more to do with his recovery than I did – but Gordon was not to be dissuaded. Ever since he recovered, he would visit me every year around Christmas and bring me the gift of a desk diary for the New Year, a tradition he kept up for the many years he lived after his initial diagnosis.

Many people leave tokens and mementos such as these at the Cruz de Fero, the highest point on the Camino – but when I saw the unsightly pile of stones, crucifixes, cards, fading notes written on paper, photographs and ribbons at the foot of the Cruz, I decided that I would carry the pebbles further on with me until I found a suitable place to lay them to rest. Over the past few days I had been wondering where I would leave them.

At the Plaza de Obradoiro Shivantha and I had been lying on our backs on the plaza, knees drawn up and propped up on our forearms and elbows, gazing up at the façade of the Cathedral - when I felt something fall out of my pocket.

It was the black stone.

Nothing else fell out – not my coins, not the white pebble, not my pen. It was almost as if Gordon Brown had decided that this was where 'his' stone, picked up at the start of my Camino and carried all the way with me along my journey, should rest – in front of the Cathedral in Santiago.

Was it a chance happening? I think not.

And I then made a decision that I would not leave here in Santiago the white pebble I had picked up in St Jean Pied de Port and carried along this journey for my mother. I would keep it with me until I went back to *Lakmahal* in Sri Lanka, to the home where my mother had given birth to me and where during my growing years she had looked after me – and in later years, Shivantha. I would place it in the same garden where I remember as a small child she would sit with me on a mat and read to me in the evenings. That would be a more fitting tribute to her than depositing it in Spain.

Later on we walked to the pilgrim office to queue up to get our *Compostelas*, the certificates that proved we had walked the

Camino. The two of us had time for a relaxed beer seated at a table on one of the streets leading on to the plaza. We didn't talk much, just taking the time to enjoy the moment, quietly soaking in and savouring the pleasant feeling of our success.

There were exchanges of greetings with those we recognised from our encounters at various times along our journey, for there were quite a few who remembered meeting the 'father and son who were walking together'. Afterwards we attended (still in our grubby pilgrim clothes) the 7 pm pilgrims' mass where we witnessed the famous *Botafumeiro* in motion. On the way back to the *albergue* we stopped for dinner at the Navroz restaurant run by a father and son from Kurdistan, where for the first time we tasted an unusual Kurdistani dessert – which was delicious.

Friday 3rd June 2011: Santiago de Compostela

We slept soundly despite being packed in like New York commuters in a rush hour train. Leaving the Albergue Acuario we walked to the Hotel San Lorenzo on the north side of the city which I had booked on the internet last night. Having checked in, showered and changed, we got into clothes a bit better than the pilgrim garb in which we attended the mass last evening and walked back to the cathedral for the 12 o'clock pilgrims' mass.

At every midday pilgrims' mass the priest always reads out the numbers and countries of origin of the pilgrims who had arrived the previous day and claimed their *Compostelas* – and we were quite pleased and proud to hear him read out from his list, "*Dos peregrinos de Sri Lanka*" (two pilgrims from Sri Lanka). A highlight of the service was the magnificent spectacle of the *Botafumeiro*, the giant silver incense burner or thurible (at 80 kg one of the largest in the world) that is swung in a huge arc from the ceiling. The melodious singing, led by a nun with the most beautiful voice, was profoundly moving.

After the service we explored the cathedral, stopping as tradition has it to hug the statue of Santiago *('uno abrazo por Santiago'* – a hug for St James*)* and then walked down into the crypt below the altar where the purported remains of the patron saint of Spain were interred. Some around us were deeply emotional – one woman even in tears – as they laid eyes on the relic casket.

Does the casket really contain the bones of St James? Does the jewelled casket at the Dalada Maligawa in Sri Lanka actually contain the tooth relic of the Buddha – or the shrine in Kashmir the hair of the Prophet Mohamed? These are not matters that can be tested or proved – but does it really matter? As long as men believe, that is all that counts, because it is faith that makes these beliefs whole.

I gaze on the silver casket that was the inspiration for so many over the years to have made the long, arduous and dangerous journey to this place of worship. I am well aware that I am a foreigner in this place – not a Spaniard, not even a Catholic – but I feel a deep sense of belonging. I bow my head and pay my respects to Santiago not as a devout Christian pilgrim but simply as a humble and reverent heathen who is thankful that he and his son completed this journey safely – and benefited so much from the experience.

Afterwards the two of us walked back to Hotel San Lorenzo and sat in the garden of the bar next to our hotel. Over a couple of glasses of wine we spent a long time reminiscing about the events of the last 45 days since we had met up in the Hotel Millenium in Paris.

It had been a long walk to Santiago – and we had learned. as T. S. Eliot said: 'It is the journey not the arrival that matters.'

Chapter 11: Reflections

Many of my middle-aged friends, colleagues and patients with whom I have shared the story of my Camino have told me, "I wish I could do something like that with my own son, but..."

I have come to understand that most fathers and sons nurture an unspoken yearning for a closer bond with each other – but being stereotypically male and congenitally endowed with the emotional range of drone bees, we have difficulty expressing this need to each other. A lot of men, by the time they reach my age, often feel trapped in their careers and tied down to their jobs – jobs which are like tunnels with no light at the end. If at all we do glimpse a light at the far end of the tunnel, it is probably the light of the express train that is coming towards us, getting faster and faster, to finally mow us down. If truth be told, we have allowed ourselves to be caught up in the grip of the fast-flowing river of life that is inexorably taking us to those inevitable destinations of exhaustion, retirement and death.

And taking time out from one's job – even two months – is a most unorthodox thing to do. Sure, I had a spell of sabbatical leave from the university, and a head of department, Professor Leon Piterman, who understood and approved of my idea of spending this time walking across Spain instead of undertaking a research project in some faraway university. But I had to also take leave from my clinic – and since I would not be available to see patients during this time I would lose income for the period that I would be away. Would what I was going to lose financially be made up for by what I would gain spiritually and emotionally?

And what about the other human being involved in this enterprise – my son? Was he as keen on spending this time with his father as I was to spend it with him? I had my answer one evening in Villafranca del Bierzo as we sat in the evening sun on a bench by the Rio Burbia, finishing the bottle of wine that we had bought to accompany the chorizo, *pimientos*, cheese and tinned *zamburinos* that made up our dinner. He suddenly turned to me and said, "You know, *Thaththi*, I can't think of any of my friends' fathers or my father's friends who would take the time off their work to do this Camino with their sons."

While travel is reputed to broaden the mind – and also lighten the purse – I firmly believe that traveling along the Camino, on foot with my son, was one of the best things I have done in my life.

People undertake a journey along the Camino for a variety of reasons. Some do it to mark retirement, some to fill the gap between studying and starting their first job, and others, faced with some turning point in their lives, set off on the Camino to take time out to decide what they should do next. Others take it on as a challenge of physical fitness, stamina and achieving a predetermined goal measured in terms of distance and time. There are yet others who do it in memory of a departed loved one – and I dare say there are still some who do it with a view to obtaining an indulgence and forgiveness of at least some of their sins.

Walking in company allows you to meet folk from different parts of the world and different walks of life – folk you would never have met if not for the Camino. You will make contact, you will connect and perhaps even develop friendships that will last long after you have completed your Camino. Walking alone you have time to think, to reflect and to contemplate on things that the rat race of modern life does not provide you with either the time or inclination to do. Walking with a spouse or parent or child provides you with an opportunity to reconnect and share time together without the constant interruptions of the householder's existence.

It is often said that one is changed by 'Walking the Camino'. This is certainly true – whether the change is a drastic one or a more subtle change in one's outlook or values or attitude to life. Perhaps the change is acquired by what one learns along the way – to strip away the non-essentials, leave behind unnecessary baggage that only serves to drag you down, and to travel light along Life's journey. Perhaps the change is wrought by some Higher Force one believes in – or perhaps there *is* no higher force except one's own subconscious efforts. Perhaps this change is the result of those one meets along The Way, perhaps it is effected simply as a consequence of having the opportunity to be away from one's routine for four to six weeks.

I cannot explain this.

All that I can say is that 'Walking the Camino' is a wonderful experience – even if nowadays it no longer qualifies you for forgiveness of your sins.

Chapter 12: Childhood's End

15th April 2012: A Year Later

It is exactly a year since I set off on my journey to Santiago de Compostela, and I ask myself – what has changed? Have I, as is predicted of those who walk the Camino, really been changed by *my* Camino?

In one sense I have changed in my outlook because completing the Camino has given me confidence – in both myself and in my son. I have also been told by my wife that I appear to have become a spiritually better person – and I am inclined to agree with her. The journey had taught me another Camino Lesson.

Camino Lesson Number Ten: ***On the Camino, as in Life, your perspective will shift and your focus will change. Things that always seemed important just won't seem that important anymore – and you will realise that worrying over things you cannot change is simply wasted energy.***

Having completed a six-week, 800 km walk over the hot *mesetas* and the cold mountains of Spain with no major problems, I have realised that despite my strong family history of diabetes and heart disease and my advanced age, I am physically more fit than I had given myself credit for – and fitter than most men my age.

I guess I must be thankful for my years in the Sri Lankan and Australian Army Reserve – and be particularly thankful to the Australian Army, who allowed me to use Army-issued boots, ponchos and backpacks that were so comfortable and yet tough. My boots were so good that I suffered neither blisters nor twisted ankles along the trail. The fact that I prepared myself thoroughly for this walk, training in earnest from the beginning of the year, would also have helped my injury-free Camino.

Camino Lesson Number Eleven: ***Prepare thoroughly, select good footwear, break in your footwear carefully – but take the journey slowly, walking at your own pace rather than racing for a deadline. Never try to push yourself beyond your capability.***

And Camino Lesson Number Twelve: ***Learn to trust yourself, and to believe that somehow, you have all that you need to make it to your destination. Have faith that you will always get to where you want to go.***

Despite this new awareness of my physical capabilities, however, I have also become keenly aware that, just because I have done the Camino, I am not invulnerable or even immune to injury or illness. Far from it! Death can strike when one least expects it, as it did Geoff's father-in-law Enrico who had walked the Camino so many times before. The Camino has taught me again that the one thing we can be certain about is the uncertainty of life.

The other change in my attitude is that I have acquired tremendous confidence in my son. Walking those long hours with him, observing him handling various situations that arose during our journey and spending so many evenings in his company allowed me to realise that the baby I carried, the toddler who used to sit astride my neck and pretend that I was his elephant steed, is now a grown man who is as capable as (in fact more capable in many ways than) his father. He has over the years developed the resources and personality – as well as a sense of fairplay and compassion – that will help him to make his way in life. I as his father can rest assured – and be grateful.

If I might paraphrase T. S. Eliot's words from his poem 'Little Gidding':

> '...*And the end of our exploring*
> *Will be to arrive where we started*
> *And know this person for the first time.*'

There were many times while we were walking that one of us noticed some sight or event that initiated a thought – an association of ideas or triggering of some memory – and when that one of us then started talking about this to the other of us, the latter would look up in surprise and exclaim, "But that is exactly what I was thinking about!"

If it was me responding, I would exclaim, "That's amazing!", while the same amazement would be expressed by Shivantha as "That's weird!"

Same difference.

My son and I have similar views on some matters and radically different views on others – but I have come now to understand that parents pass on to their children, through the nature of genes and the nurture of upbringing, common patterns of thought processing and shared memories.

This journey along the Camino has left both father and son with many happy memories of people and places. Together we met and interacted with so many folk along this journey – folk with whom we felt so oddly aligned, united in a common quest as it were – and whom we would never see again. Our slow pace of travel allowed us to enjoy the variety and natural beauty of the region – the majestic Pyrenees, the rolling vineyards of the Rioja, the forest-clad hills east of Burgos, the unrelenting flatness of the wheat fields of Castille, the snow-capped peaks of the Cantabrian mountains, the sparsely populated hill country of the Maragatos, the almond blossoms of the Bierzo valley and the Irish mists and greyness of Galicia.

And having walked the Camino I find that back in my own home now, when oft I lie in vacant or in pensive mood, I see in my mind's eye sunlight dappling on a stream trickling underneath an ancient stone bridge – or a windswept view of the Pyrenees – or an ochre path stretching out into the far distance through flat fields of wheat. I recall evenings spent in the company of strangers who became family for a night - having dinner by candlelight at the Albergue San Nicolas, enjoying a twilight singsong with a group of fellow pilgrims in the lawn of the Albergue San Mamed de Camino or just sitting with Shivantha in the evening sun on a bench by the river in Villafranca del Bierzo and enjoying our simple meal of tinned *zamburinos*, olives, bread, fruit and wine. I remember the kindness of strangers – the lady in Ventosa who bought bread and milk for us and refused payment, the English couple Ian and June from Devon at the albergue in Navarette who cooked a meal and shared it with us, the optometrist in Carrion de Los Condes who fixed my broken specs without charging me a cent for her service as well as the lady in the car outside Fromista who stopped when she saw us on the N-611 highway, and our friend Jasek who came walking after us, to point us back on to the correct path. And we still keep in touch with friends who we would never have met if not for the Camino – Roland in Lyons, Fadi in Paris, Leonie in Brisbane, Greg and Geoff in Canada.

On the other side of the coin, I realised that not everyone who comes on the Camino comes with the same intentions that we - and the majority we met - did. The persons who helped themselves to my camera in Roncesvalles, those whom we witnessed displaying intolerance or resentment of others journeying along the path – there are certainly folk who have not been stirred by the undertaking of this journey to discard uncompassionate behaviour towards others. One cannot be naïve

– just as in life, there are some who are travelling on the Camino with unwholesome motives. I do not dwell or consciously try to remember these folk and incidents – but I am aware of them.

The big cities like Leon and Burgos I found impressive, the smaller ones like Astorga and Ponferrada were delightful, there were many little towns and villages that were decidedly quaint. The views on the mountains, whether in the Pyrenees, in Galicia or looking across to the Cantabrian hills, were breathtaking.

But none of these places is so extraordinarily beautiful that it holds you back. The Camino itself is beautiful enough to keep you walking, and looking back I realise that The Way was, in fact, our destination.

Having spent six weeks walking 800 km and enjoying the journey, I must confess that arrival in Santiago was a bit of an anti-climax. Hape Kerkeling says in his book, '*When we reach our destination, it's all over. The essence of pilgrimage is of course the journey itself*'– and Theresa Burkhardt-Fuller puts it in very simple terms: '*Walking the Camino is like reading a good book. You cannot wait to reach the end and find out the ending – and then you are sorry that you have finished it!*'

And I must confess that my outlook on institutionalised religion has changed. Overexposure to the legends on the Camino has made me question the very myths that were passed on to us in childhood as gospel truth. Santiago appearing on a white horse in the sky to descend on to the battlefield at Clavijo and kill Muslim soldiers, Santiago dressed in pilgrim's garb and wending his way along the Camino to his own grave to pay his respects to his own headless body, the roast chicken that rose from the dead and flew off the sheriff's dinner plate in Santo Domingo de Calzada, the bread and wine in O Cebreiro that turned into flesh and blood – all these stories are, as *Star Trek*'s emotionally detached Mister Spock would have said, "Not logical". Over the centuries, conscientious priest-craft has kept them alive – and even in this 21st century there are still many who believe them to be true.

And what of the discovery of the lost relics of the dead saint in the northwestern corner of Spain, 800 years after he was decapitated in Judaea? The 'authentication' of these bones in the absence of forensic analysis and DNA testing as those of James the Apostle by the King and the local Bishop (who would both have shrewdly realised the value of acquiring a saint for the people and a shrine for the region) smacked to me of political expediency and opportunism. At the time that Christian Spain was fighting with its back to the wall against the Moorish invaders from the south, what more opportune moment for a holy Christian champion to appear on Spanish soil? This was a champion no less than the first cousin of Jesus himself, the pugnacious Son of Thunder. To have sustained this myth for over a thousand years – despite the fact that the skull of the beheaded saint is still believed by Christians of the Armenian sect to be buried in their cathedral of St James in Jerusalem – is certainly an admirable achievement.

One of the Medici Popes, Leo X, is reputed to have stated, "It has served us well, this myth of Christ." Whether Pope Leo actually made this statement is still disputed. Looking at the Christian settlements established over the years in northern Spain by people drawn to the shrine of St James, and the thousands of modern pilgrims who contribute each year to the economy of the lands around the Camino, one could not help feeling that a similar observation could well be made by the rulers of Spain ancient and modern: *"It has served us well, this myth of Santiago."*

Appendix I: Our Camino Lessons

What have we, father and son, learned by walking the Camino?

Listed below are what we describe as our 'Twelve Camino Lessons':

- Lesson Number One: ***Live in the moment. Enjoy what you have the good fortune to be doing. Don't spend every moment of the present planning how to achieve some future pleasure – just enjoy the pleasure of the present.***

- Lesson Number Two: ***No enterprise is too difficult to accomplish as long as you take it slowly. Take one small step after another and constantly keep your main objective in sight.***

- Lesson Number Three: ***Not everyone who comes on the Camino comes here with good intentions. Remember the old saying: 'Trust in God – but make sure to tether your camel.'***

- Lesson Number Four: ***Along the Camino – as along the journey of Life – be ever prepared to help a stranger in distress. Even those who may reject your initial offer of assistance can be helped.***

- Lesson Number Five: ***When disaster strikes, instead of looking at what you can no longer do, look instead at what you now have the opportunity to try. Change your perspective -- and the limitations that have been imposed on you become an incentive to seize new opportunities.***

- Lesson Number Six: ***Take your time, make sure you do not forget to rest and relax and enjoy your surroundings – and the journey will take care of itself. The pleasure of walking to Santiago is as much in the journey as in the destination.***

- Lesson Number Seven: ***When you are faced with a situation where someone – a shop or restaurant owner, a government official, even your boss at work – treats you disrespectfully, do not be afraid to be assertive and stand up for your right to be treated with respect. It may not change the immediate situation – but the person to whom you stand up will get the message and think twice before treating with disrespect the next disadvantaged person (the next black man, the next woman, the next foreigner) that they meet.***

- Lesson Number Eight: ***Truth depends on Perspective.***

- Lesson Number Nine: ***When your body tells you to take a rest, don't keep pushing on. Listen – and obey!***

- Lesson Number Ten: ***On the Camino, as in Life, your perspective will shift and your focus will change. Things that always seemed important just won't seem that important anymore - and you will realise that worrying over things you cannot change is simply wasted energy.***

- Lesson Number Eleven: ***Prepare thoroughly, select good footwear, break in your footwear carefully – but take the journey slowly, walking at your own pace rather than racing for a deadline. Never try to push yourself beyond your capability.***

- And finally, Lesson Number Twelve: ***In Life, you can have anything that you want - but not everything. Make your choices wisely – and then make every effort to achieve it, because the Universe will help you to succeed. Learn to trust yourself, and to believe that somehow, you have all that you need to make it to your destination. Have faith that you will always get to where you want to go.***

Appendix II: Bibliography

This is not a book giving the reader advice on how to walk the Camino.

For those who would like such a book, let me recommend *A Pilgrim's Guide to The Camino de Santiago* by John Brierley – comprehensive, easy to carry and the only book that we took with us on our journey.

The Camino de Santiago in Spain is probably best known as a pilgrim way for Catholics, and if it is this religious and spiritual aspect of the Camino that you would like to read about, let me recommend two books written by Australians: Theresa Burkhardt-Felder's *Pray for me in Santiago* (Fremantle Arts Centre Press 2005 - ISBN 1 920731 45 8); and Tony Kevin's *Walking the Camino* (Scribe Publications 2007 - ISBN 9781921215445). Although I am not a Catholic, I found the former inspiring and the latter reassuring.

For those who would like to read of a non-Catholic yet profoundly spiritual journey along the Camino, there is Shirley MacLaine's book *The Camino – A Journey of the Spirit* (Pocket Books 2000 – ISBN 978-1-4165-5387-8) which inspired many Americans to walk the Camino – while *I'm Off Then* by Hape Kerkeling, one of Germany's most famous TV comedians, is said to have been the inspiration for numerous German pilgrims to undertake the trek.

For a more irreverent Australian look at the Camino, you could always have a look at Tom Trumble's *Unholy Pilgrims*

(Penguin Books (2011) ISBN 9780143205852). In my view it was too irreverent - but then tastes differ, and you may find that in your view it is an invigorating read.

My own book, in contrast to all of the above, is simply a tale about a middle-aged man who, much to the surprise of his colleagues and friends, took six weeks off a busy medical practice to spend this time with his adult son walking from one end of Spain to the other. It was a once in a lifetime journey along an 800 km trail that meandered through hamlets, villages, towns and cities, along mountain tracks as well as through the flat hot *meseta*. It was a journey that was physically demanding and spiritually challenging - but something that turned out to be one of the best experiences of my life.

This journey of a lifetime – this long walk with my son - just happened to be along the thousand-year-old pilgrim trail known as the Camino de Santiago.

Books we found useful:

1. **Best, Elizabeth and Bowles, Colin. *The Year we Seized the Day***

    - Allen & Unwin (2007) ISBN 978-1-74237-295-2

    - 83, Alexander Street, Crows Nest, NSW 2065, Australia.

2. **Brierley, John**. ***A Pilgrim's Guide to the Camino de Santiago.***

    - Findhorn Press Ltd (2009) ISBN 978-1-844409-156-0

    - 305a, The Park, Findhorn, Forres IV36 3TE, Scotland, UK

3. **Burkhardt-Felder, Theresa**. ***Pray for me in Santiago***.

    - Fremantle Arts Centre Press (2005) ISBN 1 920731 45 8

    - 25 Quarry Street Fremantle. North Fremantle 6159, Australia.

4. **Emilio Estevez. *The Way*** Movie (2011)

5. **Faine, Jon and Faine, Jack. *From Here to There***

    - HarperCollins Publishers (2010) ISBN 978-0-7333-2387-4

    - 25 Ryde Road, Pymble Sydney NSW, Australia

6. **Hitt, Jack. *Off the Road***

   - Simon and Schuster Paperbacks (2005) ISBN0743261110
   - 1230 Avenue of the Americas, New York NY 10020 USA

7. **Kevin, Tony. *Walking the Camino.***

   - Scribe Publications (2007) ISBN 9781921215445,
   - PO Box 523, Carlton North, Victoria, Australia

8. **Koontz, Kurt. *A Million Steps***

   - Koontz (2013) ISBN 978-061585-292-8
   - Lexington, KY USA

9. **Kerkeling, Hape. *I'm Off Then: Losing and Finding myself on the Camino de Santiago*** (English translation)

   - Simon & Schuster (2009) ISBN 978-1-4165-5387-8
   - 1230 Avenue of the Americas, New York NY 10020 USA.

10. **MacLaine, Shirley. *The Camino. A Journey of the Spirit***

    - Pocket Books (2000) ISBN 978-0-7434-0073-2,
    - 1230, Avenue of the Americas, New York NY 10020 USA

11. **Manwaring, Karen. *A Slow Walk Across Spain***

    - Watermelon Press (2010) ISBN 978-0-646-54465-6

12. **Mullen, Robert. *Call of the Camino***

    - Findhorn Press (2010) ISBN 978-1-84409-510-0
    - 117-121, High Street, Forres IV36 1AB, Scotland, UK.

13. **Sheen, Martin and Estevez, Emilio *Along The Way***

- Simon & Shuster (2012) ISBN: 978-1-849836-96-8
- 1230 Avenue of the Americas, New York NY 10020 USA.

14. **Thatcher, Guy. *A Journey of Days.***

- General Store Publishing House (2008) ISBN 978-1-897113-99-8
- 499, O'Brien Road, Renfrew Ontario, K7V 4A6, Canada

15. **Trumble, Tom. *Unholy Pilgrims***

- Penguin Books (2011) ISBN 978-0143205852,
- 250 Camberwell Road, Camberwell, Victoria 3124, Australia

16. **Tuffield, Lois. *Do You Know the Way?***

- CreateSpace Independent Publishing Platform (2013) ISBN 978-149-289-6784